I
ONLY
WANT
TO GET
Married
ONCE
ONCE

CHANA LEVITAN

I ONLY WANT TO GET *Married* ONCE

Dating Secrets for Getting It Right the First Time

gefen
publishing house
JERUSALEM ◆ NEW YORK   Est. 1981

Cover Design and Typesetting by S. Kim Glassman

ISBN: 978-965-229-498-2

1 3 5 7 9 8 6 4 2

Gefen Publishing House, Ltd.   Gefen Books
6 Hatzvi Street   600 Broadway
Jerusalem 94386, Israel   Lynbrook, NY 11563, USA
972-2-538-0247   1-800-477-5257
orders@gefenpublishing.com   orders@gefenpublishing.com

www.gefenpublishing.com

Printed in Israel   *Send for our free catalogue*

This book is dedicated

to

my husband Aryeh,

with whom it is a true privilege
to travel the journey of life.

The stories in this book are about real people and their lives. However, all names and some details have been changed to protect the identities of the individuals involved.

CONTENTS

by
Sharon Slater, Psy.D.
Clinical Psychologist

Ten years ago, I received a call from a young woman named Dana who had broken off her engagement a mere two weeks before she was supposed to walk down the aisle. The wedding date itself had just passed, and Dana had spent the day in tears, wondering if she would ever find the right man and worrying about making a similar mistake in the future. When she started coming to therapy, it became immediately clear that her decision to end the engagement had been a smart one.

Dana described her relationship with Steve as a whirlwind romance. He looked like Pierce Brosnan, only twenty years younger, and had a job in the Secret Service. He was the strong, silent type, someone she could always lean on. He was the only son in a family of daughters, and had a close, warm relationship with his parents. Within four months, the couple was engaged.

Then problems began to surface. Although Steve's job sounded exciting on paper, the reality was that he needed to be available at a moment's notice, might disappear for days at a time, and couldn't share any details of his whereabouts. Steve's "manly" demeanor, which was initially so attractive to Dana, made it very difficult for the two to communicate. Steve was quiet and introverted by nature, a man of few words. Although he listened attentively when Dana analyzed and discussed issues at length, he rarely responded, and was not particularly in touch with his emotions. Socializing was also difficult because Dana loved making plans with other couples, while Steve preferred quiet nights at home. What's more, as Dana got to know Steve's family, she realized that his "close" relationship with his parents was actually a controlling one. He was incapable of standing up to them. As the wedding date approached, it became glaringly obvious that the relationship was destined for failure, so Dana finally called it off.

What concerned me most after hearing Dana's story was that she had no clear understanding of where she had gone wrong. How did she miss that they were such a poor match? An honors graduate of an Ivy League university, she was obviously very intelligent and she was also socially adept. The problem was that when she started dating, she stopped using her brain. My goal was to help Dana learn to trust her judgment again and to recognize the common pitfalls in relationships.

I've had numerous clients tell me about bad relationships that they stayed in despite obvious warning signs. They ignored feedback from family and friends, allowed major problems to slide by without addressing them, and suppressed that inner voice that was yelling "Break up!" Too many people end up in these damaging relationships simply because they don't have the relationship tools and knowledge to choose a partner wisely. Sadly, some of my clients didn't realize their mistake until it was too late and divorce was the only option.

Chana Levitan has successfully prevented many people from going through this type of heartache. For 22 years, she has been educating, mentoring, and enlightening people about how to find real potential in their relationships. Her classes on the topic are standing-room only. Chana Levitan has also had countless one-on-one conversations with thousands of single women and men about how to size up their relationships and identify real issues. I've personally worked with numerous couples who, based on her guidance, have reached a decision to marry, or sometimes, to separate and seek other, healthier relationships.

With this book, Chana Levitan is finally sharing her knowledge with a bigger audience. You'll find a smart, clear relationship guide with 10 essential questions that need to be asked before – and during – the dating process in order to spot long-term potential. Filled with real-life anecdotes and insightful dating advice, these chapters will help you better understand yourself and what you really need to succeed in building a loving marriage.

There is no rule that heartbreak must be a prerequisite for good judgment. *I Only Want to Get Married Once* will help you get it right the first time and gain the confidence to steer through the decision-making process of dating.

ACKNOWLEDGMENTS

*T*his book would simply not exist today if not for my friend and colleague Dr. Sharon Slater. It was Sharon's constant prodding, encouragement, and eventual push that convinced me to write this book. If that weren't enough, her devoted support continued throughout the book's evolution, and is still going strong.

Special thanks to Mrs. Tzipporah Heller, mentor, friend, and colleague, for the countless hours she spent poring over my manuscript, lending brilliant insights and suggestions; to my superb editors, Ita Olesker and Sarah Glazer, for lending their extraordinary editing abilities to my manuscript and for showing me that editing is a true art; and to John Sharp, who saw the potential in my manuscript and gave it wings.

My gratitude goes to Mrs. Channa Flam for her incredible insights and ideas and for being such a valuable role model for so many young women; to Dr. Judith Mishell, for graciously adding her professional insights; to my esteemed colleague Yosef Lynn and his wife Regine, for their invaluable observations and tips; and to Gary Torgow, for diving in to assist with his usual efficient, caring and professional touch.

To all of the colleges, organizations, schools and programs that have given me so many wonderful opportunities to teach and lecture, I am eternally grateful.

I am grateful to Kimber (Sherman) Wrosh for her amazing pointers and her immediate response whenever help was needed; to Marianna Grinshpun, my computer wiz, for her round-the-clock assistance and important input; and to these incredibly savvy women for their fresh and indispensable feedback: Natasha Bangay, Yocheved Engel, Sharon Ganger, Lanie Goldenberg, Lauren Gottesman, Sara Kohn, Theresa Linsner, Megan Michaels, Shoshana Rubli and Batya Taylor.

Thanks are due to Ilan Greenfield and the entire Gefen Publishing House staff for being the most proactive, enthusiastic, and professional publishing staff around – in particular, to Kezia Raffel Pride, editor par excellence; to S. Kim Glassman, an artist of the highest caliber, for the cover, graphics, and typesetting; and to Smadar Belilty, one super-talented projects coordinator.

To all of the men and women who contributed to these pages, and to my amazing students, past and present: I hope that I am able to give to you at least a fraction of what you give to me.

I am thankful to my closest friends, Esther Solomon, Lisa Marcus, and Ivy Kalazon, for their perceptive comments and thoughtful advice regarding this book and of course, for their years of devotion and true friendship.

My profoundest thanks to my father and siblings (and my mother of blessed memory), for always being so loving and supportive; and to my in-laws, for…my husband! and for so much more; and to my cousin Elana Dvir, for her constant support and involvement in every step of this process, and in all of my endeavors.

To my husband and children: I always said that I wouldn't write the generic "Thank you for putting up with my long hours at the computer"…*but*…how can I not thank you for putting up with that crazy frenzy of putting this book into writing? And thank you for all of the love and support along the way…and always. Your smiling faces make my day, every day. Thank you for being you.

Dear Reader,

Love. Everyone yearns for it, yet so few seem to have the opportunity to bask in it, to trust it, to experience it. As Eric Fromm writes, "There is hardly any activity, any enterprise, which is started with such tremendous hopes and expectations, and yet, which fails so regularly, as love. If this were the case with any other activity, people would be eager to know the reasons for the failure, and to learn how one could do better, or they would give up the activity."[1] Over the past twenty-plus years of counseling and lecturing, I've had hundreds of women crying to me about their heartbreak, their disappointments, and their failed relationships. Although seeking love certainly brings trials that make a person constantly grow and change, this pain is in essence a healthy growing pain. Love is not the chaos, heartbreak, confusion, and desperation that we are observing today. This is not love – this is insanity.

I remember one particular story I heard that sums up the experiences of so many others. A savvy, talented young woman, who was struggling through yet another disastrous relationship, told me the following: "My brother was in town visiting, and so we went out for dinner. As we opened up about our mutual relationship train wrecks, we started connecting things back to our parents' horrible divorce. Suddenly my brother turned to me and said, 'You have the same problem that I have. Your fear of getting divorced is greater than your desire to get married.'"

Everyone knows that a car won't get very far if one foot is on the gas and one foot is on the brake. But for some reason, we fail to apply this insight in our relationships.

---

1. New York: Harper and Row, 1956; repr. London: HarperCollins, 1995, p. 4.

Someone might have one foot on the brake as the result of having watched a failed marriage, or as a result of being burned from previous dating experiences, or possibly because he or she lacks the knowledge to build a happy marriage…there are endless possibilities. People have lost their confidence – both in their ability to choose an appropriate spouse and to create a loving marriage. Many men and women are afraid to really put themselves out there. However, as the saying goes, "Ships are safe in harbor, but that's not what ships were created for."

My conviction to help people succeed in building a loving marriage, rather than getting hurt, was the impetus for years of study and research on the subject. This research and my years of counseling led me to develop a series of ten thought-provoking and penetrating questions, designed to reveal the potential in a relationship early on.

The feedback I've received is that these ten questions have been tremendously helpful in directing people to gain clarity in their relationships. Due to the overwhelming response, I felt a desire to share these questions with a larger audience. Although I am an educator of Judaic studies, the information in this book will be relevant to people of any faith. Likewise, although I have had extensive experience counseling couples and individual men, I have had that much more experience counseling women. Therefore, you will find that there are more stories in the book about women. That being said, the information in this book is just as relevant to my male readers.

I hope that this book will help you navigate your way through the dating process towards a truly enriching, loving marriage. It is my sincere wish that your heart will never again be broken.

Love: What You Need to Know

"When we sat down for coffee, I looked into his eyes and I just knew. I know that this sounds strange, but we felt each other's presence. I always felt his presence in a room…"

So, why didn't it work out?

"We tried, but he wasn't that smart. I just couldn't respect him."

"As we were walking through the park one afternoon, I suddenly felt a click. After a while we started talking so intensely that we became oblivious to everyone and everything around us. It was magical…amazing…"

So, why didn't it work out?

"She was on a different path. Eventually, we felt alone even when we were together."

"When we met, we connected immediately. I felt like I'd known him my whole life. I knew he was the one for me."

So, why didn't it work out?

"Oh…even though I was serious about him, he just wasn't ready to settle down."

Sound familiar? It's always a shock when the magic evaporates. You sit there, reflecting back, thinking – how did it all go wrong? How did I not see his wandering eye? Her less-than-brilliant comments? What made me so blind? There's a reason your vision was impaired: it's called infatuation.

What Is Infatuation?

First of all, what is infatuation? Infatuation is that intense, almost chemical connection you feel with someone. It's sudden and often catches you off guard. It might smack you in the face with someone who wouldn't be good for you in the long run; yet nonetheless, against your will, you feel an attraction. When infatuated, suddenly you don't have an appetite and it's difficult to sleep. You find yourself making foolish choices, unable to think rationally.

According to Merriam Webster's Collegiate Dictionary, to infatuate is

1. to cause to be foolish, deprived of sound judgment;
2. to inspire with foolish or extravagant love or admiration.

Why is infatuation so foolish? Because it's not based on anything real, it's filled with illusion.

So why is infatuation so powerful? Because it touches on a deep human need: the need for connection. This book is all about how to get that true, lasting connection, which deepens with time – that which we call love. In order to get there, you need to know how to see through the illusion of infatuation.

There are a few elements common to infatuation. If you can learn to spot them, you'll be able to catch yourself before the "feeling" gets the best of you.

Effortless

The first element of infatuation is that it is effortless. This is one of the reasons it is so addictive. You don't have to work for it. Infatuation doesn't begin with a conscious decision such as "Oh, he's cute! And my parents would love him... I think I'll be infatuated with him" (though life would be much easier if it worked that way). No, infatuation sneaks up on you when you least expect it. Strangely enough, it is often with the guy or girl that your parents wouldn't like. As a matter of fact, sometimes, *you don't even like the person you are infatuated with*. Ever think about that one?

There are many theories as to why you might be attracted to a particular person. Is it just desire? Is it, as Dr. Harville Hendrix writes in his book *Getting the Love You Want*, that you have some unfinished business from your childhood, which seems to correlate to the issues of the person you like?[2] Whatever the case, it is clear that you can even have feelings of attraction for someone you don't like; for someone you don't respect; for someone you don't want to have chemistry with. Yet, the feelings are so strong and compelling that it's hard to walk away.

Image Oriented

Infatuation is very image oriented. When infatuated, you get caught up in who you think the person is, or more precisely, who you want him or her to be. The spell is often broken when you learn more about the person. But until then, you are able to remain in a state of ecstasy, or perhaps one should say, imagined ecstasy.

---

2. Harville Hendrix, *Getting the Love You Want* (New York: Harper and Row, 1988).

Temporary

Infatuation is simply short-lived. Erich Fromm makes this point very clear in his book *The Art of Loving*:

> If two people who have been strangers, as all of us are, suddenly let the wall between them break down, and feel close, feel one, this moment of oneness is one of the most exhilarating, most exciting experiences in life. It is all the more wonderful and miraculous for persons who have been shut off, isolated, without love.... However, this type of love is by its very nature not lasting. The two persons become well acquainted, their intimacy loses more and more its miraculous character, until their antagonism, their disappointments, their mutual boredom kill whatever is left of the initial excitement. Yet, in the beginning they do not know all this; in fact, they take the intensity of the infatuation, this being "crazy" about each other, for proof of the intensity of their love, while it may only prove the degree of their preceding loneliness.[3]

How long might infatuation last? An hour? A day? (Sometimes it lasts until the object of your infatuation opens his or her mouth.) Some social scientists say six to eighteen months. According to Helen Fisher in her book *The Anatomy of Love: The Natural History of Monogamy, Adultery and Divorce*, "Alas, infatuation fades.... At some point, that...magic wanes. Yet there does seem to be a general length to this condition. Psychologist Dorothy Tennov measured the duration of romantic love, from the mo-

---

3. New York: Harper and Row, 1956; repr. London: HarperCollins, 1995, p. 3.

ment infatuation hit to when a 'feeling of neutrality' for one's love object began. She concluded, 'The most frequent interval, as well as the average, is between approximately 18 months and three years.'"[4]

Fisher also draws a parallel between this three-year max and the common year couples divorce. She says, "Hoping to get some insight into the nature of divorce, I turned to the demographic yearbooks of the United Nations. Divorce generally occurs early in marriage – peaking in or around the fourth year after the wedding – followed by a gradual decline in divorce as more years of marriage go by."[5] She notes, interestingly, that the American divorce peak is somewhat lower than this four-year peak. It may be connected to our American "instant gratification" society. But whatever the reason, it is clear that infatuation has proven itself to be a weak and undependable element in assessing the potential of a relationship.

Controlled by Imagination

A fourth element of infatuation is the unleashing of the imagination through obsessive daydreams and fantasies. You find yourself replaying pictures and scenes in your head. The daydreams are often about someone unattainable. Some people experience a "fantastical roller-coaster ride." It feels really good. But it also feels scary to be out of touch with reality. The fantasies take over and you become aware that you've left reality behind. And that is precisely one of the prices you pay for infatuation: you're not controlling your imagination; your imagination is controlling you. At moments such as these, people almost feel enslaved. This

---

4. New York: W.W. Norton, 1992, pp. 56–57.

5. Ibid., p. 109.

struggle of infatuation is the theme of many songs in popular culture. A few examples are Beyoncé's "Crazy In Love," Kelly Clarkson's "Addicted" and Maroon 5's song which is actually called "Infatuation." The themes of these songs and so many others are:

- Feeling and acting like a fool.
- The "spinning out of control" of your fantasies and thoughts.
- The feeling of "I'm not being me...," almost as if you were possessed.
- The inability to see the object of your infatuation for who he or she is.
- The realization that in order to grow, you have to give up the object of your infatuation.

Love, on the contrary, is rooted in knowing rather than imagining. Love is not lost in fantasy; it can take a step back, evaluate itself, and see a bigger picture. Yes, there is an element of infatuation at the beginning of love. Yes, there is some imagination, daydreaming, difficulty in sleeping, etc. However, the person is not "out of control." He or she *can* think clearly (for the most part), *can* see the other person's faults, *can* logically explain (on some level) the basis for his or her feelings, *can* act responsibly.

Selfish

Another aspect of infatuation is that it has a selfish nature. Infatuation is about how "you make *me* feel." I want to feel a certain way and I feel that way when I am with you. It is self-centered. Sure, I feel like giving when infatuated. However, if I am to be honest with myself, that giving is self-serving. I'll give as long

I am getting something. It all comes back to *me*. It reminds me of the analogy of walking through a beautiful rose garden and falling in love with a particular rose. Imagine a person saying, "I love this rose! Did you see this rose?" I love it...pluck...I just killed that rose. Wanting something for "me," on my terms, has nothing to do with love.

Love is all about giving. It's an ongoing concern with another, regardless of how that person makes us feel. It's about learning to get out of ourselves, out of our narcissism, and focusing on the other person. As the saying goes, love is all about learning to spell "Us" with a capital "You."

The real secret about the selfishness of infatuation is the following: When you're infatuated, you're not only infatuated with the object of your infatuation. In a strange way, you are also infatuated with yourself. If you think about it, you'll notice that when you're infatuated, you are seeing yourself through the other person's eyes. Because the person you're dating looks at you adoringly, you feel adorable. When he or she thinks that you are smart, you feel smart. This creates a strange dependence and an insecurity – the insecurity that tomorrow, he or she may not find you so adorable. And then you may no longer feel so adorable. Once again, it all comes back to "me."

Promotes Insecurity

Insecurity is generated by infatuation. It's something that's built into the very foundation of infatuation. When infatuated, you are thrilled, but not happy. Being thrilled is a superficial excitement or giddiness. It lacks the calm and inner comfort of happiness. The thrill of infatuation seems to be accompanied by a cloud of uncertainty hovering over one's head: the worry that tomorrow, the spell will wear off and he'll lose interest.

Six Features of Infatuation

1. Effortless
2. Image oriented
3. Temporary
4. Controlled by imagination
5. Selfish
6. Promotes insecurity

Many people confuse the experience of infatuation with the experience of love. Awareness of the above six elements will serve as a foundation for working through this confusion. The rest of this book will help you make wise choices based on this foundation.

Can Infatuation Lead to Love?

I am often asked the following question: can infatuation lead to love? Although infatuation could theoretically lead to love, often it doesn't. Why not?

Truth be told, any and every dating experience is at least partially affected by infatuation. That's why dating is so confusing. If infatuation and love had nothing to do with each other, life would be much easier. Infatuation is really meant to be *part* of the spark at the beginning of a relationship. However it can't be the foundation of the relationship.

If infatuation should be part of the spark at the beginning, the question is, how big a part? The equation of love versus infatuation works as follows: If the relationship is based on

80-100 percent infatuation, the chances are very slim that this relationship will ever mature into love. There is no foundation for love, and most people, in such a situation, won't do the work necessary in order to build love. If, on the other hand, infatuation is kept in check, if it's only 10-30 percent, there is tremendous potential for love. Why? Because when infatuation is kept in check, you are in reality. You can see the bigger picture, partly because there *is* a bigger picture.

Five Signs
Your Infatuation Is a Problem

In short, infatuation is a problem when:

1. It has become the basis for a relationship and there's nothing else there.
2. You're so affected by the natural attraction that you can't see who the person really is. Therefore, you can't make a clear and responsible choice as to whether to commit.
3. You're infatuated with someone that you know is bad for you. Therefore, being in a relationship with him or her will be self-destructive.
4. You're involved in a relationship moving towards marriage but you find yourself thinking about someone you've dated in the past.
5. You're wasting a tremendous amount of time being infatuated with and fantasizing a life with someone you could never marry.

When infatuation isn't kept in check, people are unable to see the bigger picture and end up making unwise choices. These choices often come with a price tag: a broken heart or divorce. If you're not convinced of the price tag of infatuation, you need only to turn the radio on to hear confirmation of this truth in today's culture:

from Barbra Streisand's
"No More Tears (Enough Is Enough)"
to U2's "You're So Cruel,"

from The Righteous Brothers'
"You've Lost That Lovin' Feeling"
to Rihanna's "I Hate That I Love You,"

from Jackson Browne's
"Here Come Those Tears Again"
to Maroon 5's "Better That We Break,"

the cry of a broken heart has always been a popular theme.

So yes, people most definitely pay a price for their infatuation. The illusion and excitement eventually wear off, and they are left with pain and humiliation. And then, if they stay together, what do they have to look forward to? A dull, passionless marriage?

Not if they go about things the right way! I believe in love and have personally witnessed, in hundreds of marriages, how love can keep a marriage alive, nurturing, and meaningful. But, before you learn about the power of love, you must first be clear on what love is not. Although chemistry is part of love, it is not love.

Perhaps the best way to express the relationship between love and infatuation is through a commonly used analogy: If you want to make a camp fire, you'll need a few ingredients.

A couple of good strong logs, and of course some twigs, some paper, and matches. If you attempted to kindle the logs directly, you would be there waiting all night. However, if you were to light the twigs and paper without the logs, the fire would burn bright, but last a very short time. You certainly need both the twigs and the logs.

Some infatuation (twigs) is present in any relationship, and it plays an important role in igniting the logs of love. However, you had better make sure that there are some logs in the picture as well. Otherwise, the twigs of infatuation will burn out quickly. You must make sure that infatuation is not the foundation of your relationship. When you get carried away with the chemistry, when you don't check to see if there is something else there, you usually end up brokenhearted.

The big question is this: if infatuation is part of the picture, yet it is so very tricky and so potentially destructive, how can you learn to trust yourself? Is there a way to check the love potential in a relationship early on, before you invest your time and energy, heart and soul? Is there a way to keep the infatuation in check, so that you can think clearly?

The following ten questions will help you to do just that. If you are looking to build a healthy, lasting marriage, these questions will help you check that your "love logs" are in place.

CHAPTER ONE

QUESTION #1:

Do you share the same basic goals and values?

*N*o, your grandmother did not ask me to write about this. If this question conjures up negative, ridiculously old-fashioned images, don't throw the baby out with the bathwater. Read on and you'll see that in the twenty-first century, this question is as potent as ever.

Time has proven, over and over again, that when the excitement of a new relationship starts to wear off, when those twigs burn out, one's goals and values suddenly become more glaring and obvious. No matter how great the initial chemistry is, if your values are on two different pages, the odds of your marriage working decrease significantly.

What is a "value"? In essence, values are our bedrock ideals. They are our convictions regarding what we believe is right or wrong, good or bad, important and desirable. Values express our highest priorities; they are our deepest driving forces. Most people hold specific values very close to their hearts. Values are intrinsic truths. That's why people fight for their values, and some would die for their values.

Since values are an expression of one's internal self, compromising one's values is really, on some level, a negation of self. That's why people experience so much backlash when they compromise their values. Endless studies have proven that value conflict is one of the most destructive elements in a relationship. In her well-researched book *The Unexpected Legacy of Divorce*, Dr. Judith Wallerstein sums it up succinctly: "Many people divorce because they have come to abhor the lifestyle and values of their partner."[6] The obvious question is, why aren't people more careful? Why don't we just check out our value compatibility, since this is such an explosive issue? The answer goes back to infatuation. When people are attracted, they are blinded.

People commonly fall into one of these four traps:

1. They don't know their values.

2. They're so caught up in the moment that by the time the dating couple talk "values" they are already too emotionally involved.

3. They're consciously avoiding thinking about the value conflict, because they don't want to "lose the chemistry."

4. They recognize the differences in values, but naively believe that "love can conquer all," or more correctly said, "infatuation can conquer all."

A young man named Jimmy came to me for advice. He said: "I have recently started to think seriously about my future and just how important goals and values are. I'm in the process of defining mine. I've been dating Melanie for almost two years and we've always planned on getting married. But we've never really discussed goals and values. When I brought up the subject,

---

6. New York: Hyperion, 2000, p. 209.

she got very defensive. She said, 'How am I supposed to know what my values are?'" Jimmy didn't know what to answer her. I explained to him that she didn't have to pressure herself to figure it all out *now*. She didn't need to write her "Values Thesis" on the spot. But she did need to start getting in touch with her values. Why should she get in touch with her values? I spelled out to him five benefits to defining one's values, that might inspire Melanie to start the process. (These reasons are listed on page 26.)

When Jimmy sat down with Melanie and gently discussed these points, the conversation went more smoothly. However, her next question was, "How do I get in touch with my values? Does everyone have them?"

Yes, every human being has values. Dr. Nathaniel Branden, one of America's leading experts in self-esteem, answers this question in *The Six Pillars of Self-Esteem*. He writes, "A concern with morality or ethics arises naturally, in the early stages of our development.... Inherent in our existence and humanity is the question: What kind of being should I seek to become? By what principles should I guide my life? What values are worth pursuing?"[7] As we get better in touch with ourselves, we get more in touch with these values. Some of us have to think about them more consciously, some of us inherently feel them very strongly.

On December 17, 2006, the *New York Times* featured a very popular article entitled "Questions Couples Should Ask (Or Wish They Had) Before Marrying." The article begins by saying that "relationship experts report that too many couples

---

7. New York: Bantam Books-Random House, 1994, p. 39.

fail to ask each other critical questions before marrying."[8] Of the fifteen questions mentioned in the article, almost all of them are value/goal oriented. The main topics the questions cover are:

1) Bringing up children

2) Financial obligations and goals, including spending and saving money

3) How the household will be run

4) Spiritual beliefs and needs

5) How much religious/moral education for the children

6) Boundaries with in-laws

7) Where to live

8) Commitment to the marriage bond

In the same edition of the *New York Times*, Eric Copage wrote an article entitled "Marriage Is Not Built on Surprises," where he says, "For too many couples, the spouses-to-be assume that they know each other and the ground rules for their marriages, experts say. And sometimes those heading to the altar dodge important questions because they don't want to rock the boat."[9]

A perfect example of this is Daniel, a middle-aged man who was very serious about getting married. He approached me for some assistance with dating. Early on in the conversation, I asked him what his goals and values were. He responded enthusiastically, "I am so glad that you asked me that question!"

---

8. *New York Times*, December 17, 2006.

9. Ibid.

When I asked him to explain his excitement, he told me his story. Daniel's first marriage had lasted only two years. Although he and his ex-wife dated each other well over a year before getting married, and even though they had spent a lot of time together, they hardly spoke of goals and values. They were simply too busy having fun. The only "serious" discussion they had lasted a few minutes. It went something like this:

"Do you want to have kids one day?"

"Yeah...do you?"

"Yeah."

Then she asked him about his remote interest in religion.

"Do you think that you would become more religiously involved in the future?"

His answer was "I don't know."

That was the extent of the "serious" conversation. Nothing was said about how soon into the marriage they wanted to have kids. Nothing was clarified about how serious his interest in religion was. Nothing was said about her own issues with religion.

Once the couple were married, these issues quickly rose to the surface, and they started to argue about when to start a family. They had completely different visions in this area. Every time he picked up a book about religion, she became extremely anxious and started badgering him with ridiculing questions. Their marriage crashed quickly and painfully.

In order to create a solid foundation in a relationship, you need to spend some quality time trying to figure out your values, if you haven't already done so. Here is a list of values you might identify with. (Although you might identify with many or even most of these values, try to pick out your top five. These are your essential values.)

1. Loyalty
2. Integrity/Honesty
3. Hard work and discipline
4. Being knowledgeable
5. Family/Family values
6. Treating one's parents with respect
7. Commitment to one's spouse and/or children
8. Religious commitment
9. Communication
10. Following through (doing what you say)
11. Care and/or adoption of orphans
12. Accountability
13. Sincerity
14. Gratitude
15. Community service
16. Personal growth
17. Peace
18. Visiting the sick
19. Efficiency
20. Success
21. Frugality
22. Privacy
23. Justice
24. Compassion
25. Helping the disabled
26. Care for the environment
27. Devotion
28. Spirituality
29. Friendship
30. Excellence
31. Commitment to taking care of one's health
32. Hospitality
33. Volunteering
34. Positive attitude
35. Tradition
36. Meaning/Purpose
37. Respect for others
38. Changing the world
39. Leadership
40. Perseverance

Eight Questions
to Help You Define Your Values

1. What are the three most important values you would want to give your children? You must limit your answer to three!

2. List the top five areas into which you invest your time and energy. Ask yourself why.

3. What do you think are the three most important character traits that every person should develop?

4. Name three role models in your life. What is it about them that you look up to?

5. If you suddenly inherited $10 million for the strict purpose of donating it, what causes would you choose?

6. What are four things that you would want said about you in your eulogy?

7. List four values without which a part of you would die.

8. Name three of the most memorable experiences in your life; what values do these experiences conjure up?

What's the Difference between Interests, Values and Goals?

Figuring out your values, and your deeply held convictions, will also help you to clarify your goals. (Although interests are important, they play a less influential role, after values and goals.) The relationship between the three is as follows:

What is the difference between values and goals?

Your *values* are the foundations upon which your goals and dreams are built. Therefore, your values are more essential than your goals. Your *goals*, in turn, are more essential than your *interests*. Remember what was clarified above: values are essential to who you are. It is important not to deny these essentials, so as to avoid the backlash of value conflict. This means that if a couple share a common goal – for instance, they both want to start a business – but simultaneously their underlying values clash, chances are that the shared goal will not be strong enough to hold them together.

Take, for another example, Susan, who came to speak with me about a relationship into which she had invested many years. She and her boyfriend always had hopes that their relationship would one day turn into a happy marriage. They spoke about marriage, but they were young and too busy to think about "details." When they were approaching their late twenties, they began to speak seriously about marriage. All of a sudden, things looked different. Certain details they had regarded as unimportant when they first started dating now became very significant issues: the fact that they belonged to two different religions, and the fact that they came from different countries (each wanted to live in his or her own birth country).

Both had spent time living in each other's country, trying it out. Both came to the conclusion that they hated living in the other's country. But if that was the only issue, it possibly could have been worked out. The bigger issue was religion. Susan told me that when she was younger, she hadn't cared that he had a different religion. She wasn't particularly religious, so what did it matter? But now, she realized that she wanted the father of her children to share and impart religious values, teachings, and beliefs similar to those with which she identified. Her boyfriend, though, had his own set of values and religious identity. They just couldn't see eye to eye. Susan was shocked that after all these years, all of a sudden, this "detail" became so important. She was surprised that such strong feelings of religious identity were welling up within her, and within her boyfriend as well. (She's lucky; most of the time people realize this only after marriage. It usually hits them upon becoming parents.)

Susan began to see that it was the common interests and less significant goals that had held them together until now. The fact that they shared the same profession and eventually saw kids in the picture could no longer outweigh the "big stuff." Although they shared common interests (art and travel), it wasn't a strong enough foundation for building a marriage. As painful as they knew the breakup would be in the short term, they understood that the long-term pain, frustration, and anger would be many times greater, were they to marry.

People often make the mistake of thinking that if they have a few common interests and a couple of common goals, that's enough. What they don't realize is that if the commonality is on a superficial level, it's not enough. A highly intelligent woman once told me, "This is going to sound strange, but after being in a relationship with a particular man for a year, I realized one day that the only thing we had in common was that we both liked Chinese food." Why did it take her a whole year to realize this? Once again, when the attraction is strong, all too often, people stop using their heads.

Another woman, Julie, once consulted with me after a class I had given on this subject. She had just met a wonderful young man. She was very excited and felt that she might have met the right one. Julie told me, "I heard everything that you said today. I totally agree that values and goals are the most important things. I know that you also said that it is very difficult to find someone who shares all of our interests, and you warned us not to hold out for perfection. But this man I'm dating shares *all* of my interests. It's uncanny!"

I told her that such a thing was very unusual, but if it were true, she was very lucky. A couple of weeks later, Julie approached me with the following question: "What do you do if you share all of your common interests but there is a big mismatch in the value area?"

I replied, "It sounds like you spent a little more time dating him."

She laughed. It turns out that although they really did share all of their common interests, his approach to life and basic values were conflicting with hers. Their excitement about all of their shared interests camouflaged their more basic lack of compatibility.

In his book *Should We Stay Together?* Dr. Jeffry Larson lists the factors that predict marital dissatisfaction based on twenty years of his own research.[10] As far as a couple's traits are concerned, the number-one factor for marital dissatisfaction is dissimilarity. Similarity does not mean that you both like Indian food. Similarity does not mean that you agree on every topic and never have a difference of opinion. It *does* mean that the more profound and essential the similarities, the greater the potential for lasting happiness. This translates into values and goals, because those are the most profound and essential similarities.

I know of a happily married couple who actually share *no* common interests. Zero! I have never heard of a couple who are less compatible than they are. One likes sports, the other can't stand sports. One likes nature, the other hates nature. When it comes to politics, they have completely opposing views. They have different views on how to discipline the kids, how to spend vacation time…you name it. Sounds crazy, but they are actually happily married. How? The reason is that they have two things in common, two major values:

1. They don't believe in divorce and they both do everything it takes to make the marriage work.

2. They value and believe in giving. Every day they spend quality time finding ways to give to each other.

This couple is living proof of the power of shared values.

---

10. Jeffry H. Larson, *Should We Stay Together?* (San Francisco: Jossey-Bass, 2000).

We can contrast them with another couple I know who dated for a very, very long time. In the beginning of their relationship, he told her that he was not marriage oriented. They continued their relationship, which was built on many common interests and the fact that they had a great social life together. However, they differed on one particular (and very important) value. Simply put, she wanted to get married, but for him, marriage was not on the map. Some time later (when she was 37 years old), she asked him, "So, when are we going to get married? We've been dating for a long time."

He answered her, somewhat puzzled, "But I told you when we started our relationship that I never wanted to get married. I couldn't have been more clear!" He's right. She should have taken his vision more seriously, instead of thinking that she could change him.

Let's face it, it's not easy to be honest with ourselves when we have a conflict of needs. But we have to be true to ourselves, because that's the only way we will really be happy in the long run. Yes, short-term happiness feels great, but then it's gone, as quickly as it came. If your goal is lasting happiness and inner peace, then you must listen to the inner voice, the one that calls out for a reality check.

What if the person you're dating doesn't want a reality check? After one of my lectures, I was approached by a 32-year-old woman named Danielle who had been seeing Brett for nearly two years. She said, "I fully understand how important values are. I just can't get Brett to talk about them! He says, let's just enjoy each other's company, we don't need to get so 'heavy.'" We spoke about the fact that Danielle had to deal with her biological clock and the reality that investing another year in this relationship at her age would come at a very high cost.

We also spoke about Brett's fear that if there was a sober discussion of values, the infatuation would be challenged. He was afraid to lose that "feeling." Danielle realized, however, that if that "feeling" was valid, it would withstand a closer look at the inner fabric of their relationship. She concluded that since she had already invested almost two years, she deserved to have an open discussion about this inner fabric of goals and values. Danielle decided that if Brett was incapable of thinking about the future, she would have to let him go.

Although you might not want to bombard the person you're dating with "values questions" on the second date, the discussion about values and goals needs to take place sooner rather than later. A woman in her mid-30s once told me that she had signed up for a singles' dating event near her hometown. She was serious about getting married and was pleased to have been introduced to a nice guy that evening who was around her age. They hit it off, and she asked him if he would be open to answering a few questions she liked to ask men she would date. He was a good sport and immediately agreed. She took out a long list of questions she had collected over the years. As he answered her questions, she became increasingly excited. His answers were portraying exactly the man she hoped to marry. Finally, she reached the last two questions: "How do you know that you are ready to get married? Why do you want to get married?"

He answered her simply, "Who said I ever want to get married?"

Once again, it's better to clarify values sooner than later!

You have to be strong in order to make the right choices in life. It isn't easy! But the alternative – ending up with the wrong person – is far worse. If you can keep this clear in your mind and heart, you will find the strength to listen to that inner voice…the one that knows better.

Five Benefits to Defining Your Values

1. STRESS RELIEF: A major source of stress is value conflict. Clarifying and living according to your values is an essential way to diminish stress.

2. INCREASE OF FULFILLMENT: Living according to your values brings you satisfaction and fulfillment. When you honor your values, especially when it's difficult (once the discomfort passes), you will experience your integrity. There are very few things equally fulfilling.

3. EASIER DECISION MAKING: Your values are your guiding lights to determine the correctness of decisions and choices.

4. PRIORITIZATION: Having values enables you to prioritize your activities and responsibilities. This is because values determine what is most important to us.

5. CLARITY: Being clear on your values will help bring your goals, dreams, and visions into focus.

CHAPTER TWO

QUESTION #2:

*Are you relating to the person you are dating,
or to an image?*

on't worry, I'm not saying here that image is not important. You should find your potential spouse attractive,
you should feel proud to introduce him or her to your friends
and family. But sometimes, all too often, there is a tendency
to become fixated on a person's image, thus ignoring who the
person *is* underneath the image. You can become so infatuated
with who you think this person is, so taken with a particular
quality or ability of this person, that you can't see who the
person *really* is.

What do I mean by image? A few possibilities are:

1. The way a person looks
2. Profession
3. Financial status
4. Who he or she knows (rubs elbows with)
5. Reputation (i.e., where she went to university,
   or the fact that everyone says he's so brilliant
   or successful)
6. Who this person reminds us of (someone we
   like, are attracted to, etc.)

It's easy to get caught up in image. Indeed, infatuation thrives on image (while love thrives on knowledge). When you fall for someone, you can forget that people's looks change and their careers can change. You can also forget the fact that if people have money today, it doesn't mean that they will have it tomorrow. (In the Talmud, an ancient Jewish text, the coin of the day was called a *zuz*, which means "to move." This is because money has an interesting way of moving and changing owners.) You may also forget that people eventually get bored with external things, and that a relationship yearns for something deeper.

And so it happens that a person marries an image. Only afterwards comes the shock: the shock that this person is not that image and the shock of realizing that this person is so different from what you were expecting. Sometimes, a person turns out to be the very antithesis of what he or she appeared to be.

As far as looks go, yes, attraction is important, but it's not enough to sustain a relationship. In addition, people's looks change with time. Women often put on some weight with the years; men develop a belly. It is commonly said that men have three hair styles: parted, unparted, and departed. Yes, as hard as we try to fight this truth, time does affect our looks.

A person's profession is usually an important expression of identity, but a person is not only his or her profession. Underneath the title doctor, farmer, teacher, lawyer, accountant lies a person. (We hope! If not, be careful.)

A young woman named Nancy once approached me about a man she was seriously dating. He was actually her college professor but the age gap in this case was not an issue. She was very flattered by his interest in her. In addition, the tremendous bonus of this relationship was that if she married him, her future profession would be secure (she wanted to work in his field).

He had all of the connections that she would ever need. As Nancy jumped into the relationship, she was aware of a subtle voice in her head saying, "Wait a minute, do you really *like* this guy? Would you even date him if he weren't a renowned college professor?" But she was so enthralled by the fact that she had caught such a "big fish" that she didn't allow herself to listen to that voice. As weeks turned into months, the voice became louder and made her exceedingly uncomfortable. Then he asked her to marry him. By the time she came to speak with me, the voice had become a permanent pest.

As Nancy spoke about her concerns, she was able to be honest with herself. After a long discussion, she finally admitted the bitter truth: Although she was seriously considering accepting his marriage proposal, he would never have been a candidate were it not for his job. She just didn't like him enough as a person. By breaking off the relationship, she did both of them a tremendous service. Although it was hard for him to let go of her, he soon came to realize that he deserved to be in a marriage with a woman who could love him for who he really was.

Bulldozers

Some people figure, "If this person doesn't fit the image I'm looking for, I'll turn him/her into that image." It is quite common for a woman to try to change the man she is dating into her image of Mr. Cool, Mr. Serious, Mr. Scholar, etc. We all know that it is a woman's tendency to try to improve her man. However, we're not talking about improvement here. We're talking about a "makeover," an overhaul. If you feel that you need to overhaul your partner, this is a problem. I call this the "bulldozer phenomenon." Sometimes a person bulldozes into another person's life, claiming to be "helping" him or her. In reality, bulldozers are just trying to turn their potential mates into the image that they have in their heads. In essence, bulldozers don't really care about other people; they're just fixated on their own agendas.

A young woman once told me about a bulldozer in her life, a man she had dated in her past. Although they had broken up, they still had feelings for each other. A few months after their breakup, they bumped into each other at the supermarket. They both knew that there was still something there, so they decided to meet for dinner and give it a shot. They chose a beautiful restaurant to start things off right. As they sat down to their delicious meal, he told her that she was a wonderful person and that she would be even more wonderful if she lost some weight. She said, "We haven't met in a few months, and that's what you have to say to me?"

He retorted, "I just think that you'd look better if you lost some weight."

She said, "Thanks a lot!"

He responded, "I just want you to live up to your potential!"

As you can imagine, dinner ended quite abruptly. What he really meant by "living up to your potential" is "living up to my image of what my future wife should look like." Of course, people must be careful to take care of themselves and not to let themselves go (before or after marriage). The woman in the above story, however, did take care of herself. The issue was his, not hers.

Long-Distance Relationships

I cannot end this chapter without saying a word about long-distance relationships. Why do they have such a high failure rate? In the introduction, we discussed the fact that infatuation is short-lived, up to about three years. How about a crush? (A crush is a one-way infatuation. It is aptly named because it can feel crushing when the spell of infatuation is over.) How long can a crush last? Over the years, in many different countries, countless people have written about crushes that have lasted a lifetime! It's true that unrequited love can last a long, long time. But it's due to the fact that the relationship is completely in one's mind, in one's fantasies. Imagination can last forever. Since distance lends enchantment, long-distance relationships tend to have an extra amount of fantasy woven into their fabric. And long-distance relationships share an additional problem: what happens when the couple are actually in the same town? Since they know that their time together is short, their relationship tends to be very intense. When these powerful interactions are combined with emotional goodbyes, the couple's connection appears to be more real than it actually is.

International, round-the-globe dating is becoming a more common phenomenon daily. Whether people met because they happened to be in the same city for a week, or they met through one of the many national or international online dating agencies, many people find themselves dating long distance. If you find yourself in this scenario you need to know the following: No matter how great the relationship appears to be, you must spend quality time dating each other and getting to know each other in the same town. The fantasies can only be dispelled if you spend time talking and sincerely discovering who the other person really is. This includes tackling those problem areas that usually get swept under the rug.

If you're dating someone, it's essential that you take a good, serious look beneath the surface. Both you and your potential mate deserve at least that. You also want to make sure that this person is relating to *you*, not to who he or she thinks you are or want you to be. Although a person's image is important, it cannot sustain a lasting, healthy marriage. As painful as it is to admit this to ourselves, it's better to make a sober decision early on than to suffer the shock of "the mask being taken off" once it's too late.

CHAPTER THREE

QUESTION #3:

Can you admit that the person you are dating has faults? Are you realistic about your own faults?

*W*hen infatuated, you may end up convincing yourself that the object of your affection is perfect. There are typically three reasons for this:

1. You just met the person and don't know his/her faults.
2. You ignore his/her faults, or you're in denial of them. (You don't want to see the faults because it might end the infatuation.)
3. You admit his/her faults, but the infatuation is so strong that you brush them aside. It's similar to a patient after major surgery who is put on morphine. He knows that there's pain but he can't feel it. He can't access it so he doesn't have to deal with it. So too with infatuation. When infatuated, you know that the flaw is there, but you are so hooked on the infatuation that nothing seems to matter. In effect, you still see or view the object of your infatuation as "perfect."

The last tendency is especially problematic because people who are doing this actually think that they're being realistic. They admit the flaw! But they don't realize that they are on morphine. Actually, the analogy of morphine is not so far from the truth. Studies show that when a person is experiencing infatuation, a substance called phenylethylamine (PEA for short) is released into his or her system. Phenylethylamine has the potential to bring on feelings of elation, bliss, and euphoria. This substance, PEA, which is released in the brain, is also a natural amphetamine. This explains why people need so little sleep when they're infatuated.[11] So, perhaps, a person who is infatuated is literally intoxicated.

A man I once met was dating someone who had a tendency to be verbally abusive. She wasn't nasty all of the time, but sometimes she would slip, and she did so once in front of me. I told him what I had seen. He later admitted that he saw this pattern, but reassured me that he could handle it. I suggested that they get some premarital counseling, just to make sure that he could. She was opposed to the counseling, so he brushed the verbal abuse aside, deciding that it was a nonissue. He was too intoxicated with his infatuation to internalize the seriousness of her behavior. After they married, unfortunately, she continued with her abusive speech and they eventually divorced. Had he sobered up earlier, this mistake could have been avoided.

Sometimes, the person inebriated with infatuation asks the following question: isn't love all about accepting and loving a person with their flaws – in spite of their flaws? That's what I am doing! I am loving this person flaws and all!

11. Helen Fisher, *Anatomy of Love: The Natural History of Monogamy, Adultery, and Divorce* (New York: W.W. Norton, 1992), p. 57.

Tricky question. In order to find an answer, we have to remember that infatuation is effortless, while love requires some effort. The difference between how infatuation deals with flaws versus how love deals with flaws is as follows:

*   *Infatuation effortlessly ignores or plays down someone's faults.*

*   *Love consciously accepts those faults (with effort) but chooses to focus on the positive (with effort).*

Ignoring or denying someone's faults is always a recipe for trouble. Take, for example, a woman named Sarah who worked in an office with Michael. He was a good guy from her community (their parents even knew each other) and he was extremely interested in dating her. They shared so much in common that it would have been very convenient for them to date and marry. But there was one major problem. The most important, number-one thing that she needed in a future husband was kindness and sensitivity to others. Michael was a smart, successful, and ambitious man. But, he was lacking in the area of kindness and sensitivity. To Sarah, ambition and intelligence were secondary to kindness.

Michael pursued her through constant compliments and gifts. Finally, she broke down and agreed to date him. She got so caught up in the gifts that he was sending her that she paid less attention to the fact that he was rough and insensitive. When he was getting ready to propose, she found herself thinking, "I'll say yes because I feel bad saying no, especially after receiving so many gifts." At that moment, she was overcome with anxiety. How could she possibly marry Michael? With each passing day, his insensitivity was more glaring. How could she have overlooked it? How could she consider saying yes to someone's marriage proposal because she felt bad saying no?

It took a lot of strength for Sarah to be honest with herself, her family, and eventually with Michael about how she truly felt. Had she stayed focused from the beginning on the reality of his faults versus the reality of her needs, she could have avoided a very messy situation.

Once again, when we ignore that inner voice, we make a mess of things; sometimes a big mess, sometimes a small mess, but always a mess. Everyone gets hurt; no one wins. In essence, Sarah's internal voice told her early on that this relationship had no potential. We have to learn how to turn up the volume of that inner voice. It is the part of us that knows better; some call it our higher self. We all have it. The more we tune into it, the more accustomed we become to hearing it. Had Sarah listened to that internal voice, she would have taken her blinders off.

As soon as those blinders are removed, most people look back and say, "What in the world was I thinking?" A woman once said those words to me, after telling me about a horrendous relationship she had been in. When she said, "What was I thinking?" I answered her, "You weren't thinking!" Yes, we all have to pull those blinders off, activate our brains, and activate that inner voice.

Are You Realistic about Yourself?

Sometimes people are realistic about the other person but not realistic about themselves and their own faults. It's not uncommon for a woman to come to me with a list a mile long of what she wants in a future husband. Sometimes, she doesn't have many of those qualities herself. She is looking for someone out of her league. Other women underestimate themselves.

People who fail to see clearly usually fall into three traps:

1. *Infatuation.* The lie: "All I need is attraction."
2. *Desperation.* The lie: "I don't need or deserve anything," or, "There's no one else out there for me." The trap of desperation is a very dangerous one. It has caused people to ignore horrific things during the dating process.
3. *Not in reality.* The first lie: "He's perfect." The second lie: "I'm perfect" (i.e., I think I deserve more than I really deserve).

This third trap can keep a person single forever, or for a long, long time.

In order to avoid these three traps, you should do the following: Create a detailed list of the character traits you're looking for in a potential mate. (Some examples are kind, hardworking, family oriented, friendly, health oriented, strong, creative, growth oriented, funny, spiritual, efficient, etc.) Then go over the list and pick out the three most important things you need in his personality. These are your *needs*. These are the things that you cannot compromise on, no matter what. That means that if you are dating someone who clearly doesn't have one of these three character traits, you are wasting your time, as well as his. The rest of your list are your *wants*. It would be nice to get them. However, you could overlook some of them if you had everything on your needs list met. (He'll probably have character traits that you didn't even think of, which will compensate for the missing "wants.") It's highly recommended that you go over this list with a mentor. You want to make sure that you have it right.

A young man, Hal, once consulted me regarding a woman

he was dating. Neither was particularly good-looking. She really liked him; he also liked her but wasn't sure that he was attracted enough to her. Hal had already been dropped by quite a few women and was aware that he wasn't "Mr. Gorgeous." As a result, he was determined to give her a fair chance. I told him a story that my daughter had told me that very day, about a couple who were dating and liked each other very much. The one thing holding him back from marrying her was that she had a very big nose, which he found unattractive. He was open with her about this, and she said that she didn't mind getting a nose job. It was something she had always considered doing anyway. They got engaged, but there was so much to do before the wedding that she didn't have time to get her nose fixed. After the wedding, they were very busy, then she was expecting, and before they knew it, they were married for a few years with a couple of kids. One day, she decided that the time had come for her to have her nose operation, and she called the doctor to make an appointment. When she told her husband about the appointment, he was shocked. He said, "What? You're going to let someone touch that beautiful nose of yours? Please don't!"

When I finished telling Hal the story, he chuckled. A couple of weeks later, he called me to tell me that he was still dating the same woman. He then said, "I don't know what I was thinking when I said that she wasn't very attractive! She is so beautiful, I can't believe that I didn't see it right away." Hal is an example of a mature, insightful person who was real about what he deserved. This couple went on to build a very happy, loving marriage.

With All Your Flaws...

As mentioned earlier, while infatuation effortlessly ignores or plays down someone's faults, love consciously accepts those faults (with effort) but chooses to focus on the positive (with effort). So what happens in a truly loving relationship? How is it different from an infatuated one?

In a loving relationship, one with serious marriage potential, the following happens (keep in mind that there are many variations on this theme): Two people meet, they like each other, and they share certain goals, values, etc. There is attraction, but they spend time getting to know each other, going beyond the "image." As they talk and spend time together, some of their faults become more apparent. They don't ignore or deny these faults. Rather, they responsibly consider whether they can handle them. In other words, they are able to assess the authenticity of the "real-ationship" as they progress.

They build the foundation of their marriage on shared values, honesty, respect, knowledge, and yes, of course, attraction – rather than on wishful thinking, blind attraction, and a false sense of security. The relationship is built on an assessment, an understanding, and a mature acceptance of their spouses' imperfections, not a denial of them.

Anyone happily married will admit that these imperfections become more annoying at times. However, because of the strong foundation of the relationship – a relationship based on reality – the faults become less significant. They are not deliriously ignored, as they are with infatuation, as a result of being "intoxicated." They are pleasantly, and sometimes consciously, ignored and glanced over, as each spouse focuses on the positive, wonderful aspects of the other.

When you act from love, you're more likely to make responsible decisions. When you act from infatuation, you're more likely to be reckless. An example of this recklessness is the following story. I met a woman who was divorced with a few kids. When I asked her why she was divorced, she said, simply, "Because my ex-husband was abusive."

Of course my next question was, "You didn't know that he had abusive tendencies before you married him?"

To which she answered, "Of course I knew. We dated for close to two years before we got married."

My next question was even more obvious. "So *why* did you marry him?"

Her answer, unfortunately, reflects the answer many of us have heard, or said, in such a scenario. "I thought that I could handle it. I also thought that he would change after marriage."

Why do people make these types of mistakes? When people allow imagination to override better judgment, they fall. If you allow yourself to be blown away by what you like about the person you are dating, ignoring the negative, you can get into big trouble.

It is absolutely imperative that you ask yourself the following questions:

1. Can I admit the faults of the person I am dating?

2. Can I handle them?

3. Can I admit my own faults? Am I aware of my own imperfections?

4. Am I being realistic as to the type of man/woman I should marry?

5. Am I allowing my fantasies/immature needs to take over and push me to ignore negative or destructive aspects about the man/woman I'm dating?

If your answers to these questions reveal a problem area in your relationship, it's essential to speak to someone you trust: a healthy close friend, a mentor, a therapist, a family member, a clergyman, or anyone to whom you can speak freely, who can snap you back to reality. Sometimes, that's what it takes. As embarrassing as it might be to speak to someone at a moment of vulnerability, the pain of embarrassment now is nothing compared to the pain of cleaning up a mistake.

CHAPTER FOUR

QUESTION #4:

Does your relationship have healthy boundaries?

*Y*es, you want to give your all when you're dating someone, but there have to be healthy boundaries, too. How do you know if you have them? Start by reading the statements below to see if any of them sound familiar. (Note that since this issue is typically more of interest to women than to men, the examples in this chapter are generally phrased from a female perspective.)

> *Situation #1:* "At times I feel like a chameleon in relationships. I change my opinions depending on my companions. The men I date pick up on this tendency and they try to mold me into who they want me to be."

> *Situation #2:* "I broke up with this guy. I know he isn't good for me. Why do I keep going back to him when I made up my mind not to?"

Situation #3: "I feel like I have allowed my fiancé's mother to be a third party in our relationship! I mean, who is the number-one woman in his life, me or her?"

Situation #4: "I keep getting into these codependent relationships. Why can't I just have a normal relationship?" (For a definition of codependence, turn to page 57.)

Situation #5: "In the beginning, I'm always treated like a queen. Then, slowly but surely, the 'other' side comes out and I allow a man to mistreat me. I feel like a magnet for abusive men."

Many of us can identify with at least one of these statements, which are all connected to boundary issues. Once you figure out which one has been a struggle for you, you can begin to address the problem and make real changes.

Situation #1:
"At times I feel like a chameleon in relationships."

A young woman in university named Lisa once told me about how she was struggling with boundaries in her relationship:

> I always wanted to become a special-ed teacher. But the man I was dating, Simon, didn't like that profession. In the beginning, he was subtle. He would throw out lines like, "You could do big things in life. Anyone could work in special ed." Eventually Simon became more direct: "I don't want my future wife to work in such a profession. I can't relate to it." Yet he never convinced me that anything was inherently wrong with it. I felt like all he cared about was prestige and taking control of my life and my decisions. Why didn't I tell him to get lost? All my life, I've wanted to be a special-ed teacher. It's my true calling! In the end, just before I changed my major, I caught myself. I realized that I was allowing Simon to run my life. Why am I so weak? Why did it take me so long to stand up for myself? This happens a lot in my life, in different ways.

A truly happy marriage is defined by a merging of two into one. This is a concept that most people are familiar with. But the question of *how* two people are meant to become one is where people get confused. One of the misconceptions is that two become one by one person disappearing into the other person. Disappearing is not the same thing as merging. Although disappearing might appear to be closeness, it's just an illusion. Let's try to fully understand this concept.

The truth is that *two can be one...if one can be two*. This statement means that it's impossible to experience true closeness and oneness in a relationship unless both parties have a healthy self-esteem. The merging of two people into one can only happen in a healthy way if each one can stand on his or her own. If they can't, their oneness is not real oneness.

What allows a woman to lose herself in a relationship? Why might she be a chameleon depending on the person she's with? The answer is a lack of boundaries.

What is a boundary? A boundary is like a border. A border defines, contains, and protects you. You exist within your borders, and your personality grows and develops within these borders. Your borders, or boundaries, give you a sense of your own uniqueness. They say, "I have an identity." Only a person who has an identity can *contribute* to the greater whole that is formed by two becoming one, instead of one disappearing into the other person. There's a saying: "A marriage consists of two people who become one. The only problem is deciding *which* one." This saying would be funny if it weren't for that fact that so many people are actually stuck in this unhealthy type of relationship.

In Lisa's situation, she was about to give up an expression of herself that was very dear to her, for no other reason than Simon's insecurities. When she realized that she tended to allow other people to unreasonably control her and her life decisions, she knew that she had some work to do. Lisa sat down and spent quality time defining and strengthening herself. When she noticed that she had a tendency to change her opinions based on the people she was spending time with, she realized that she had to define her values and strengthen her self-esteem. She came to understand that a healthy marriage is enriched by people's differences, not threatened by them.

In order to merge, you have to know who you are. In other words, you must have a "self-concept," which means knowing what you believe in and what you stand for. Otherwise, you won't have anything to give to another person. You just *might* end up disappearing into the person you're dating. In order to assess your "self-concept," ask yourself the following questions:

1. How well do I know myself? Am I aware of my opinions? Have I thought out and developed my opinions?

2. Do I change my opinions in order to please other people? If so, are there certain types of people I do this with more? How would I describe this type of person?

3. What would I say is distinctly "me"? Who are the people in my life that appreciate this "distinct me"?

4. What are my values? My cares and concerns? My perceptions?

Answering and thinking about the answers to these questions will help you define your self-concept and develop your boundaries. No one can do this work for you. You need to discover YOU. Of course, a mentor, friend, or coach can help, but first try it on your own.

You might be wondering: "But what about growth and compromise? Everyone says that marriage is all about compromise." Yes, it's true, marriage is about compromise. The purpose of compromise is to achieve a higher goal that both people believe in. As a result, compromise cannot mean losing oneself, or compromising one's values or emotional health. Real compromise comes from the *choice* to give up something you treasure for someone you love. For example, if a woman loves Mexican food but her husband doesn't, she wouldn't always drag him to a Mexican restaurant. She would happily agree to go to his favorite steakhouse as well (obviously not sitting there grieving over her lost taco). His pleasure would authentically be her pleasure.

Healthy compromise does require giving of oneself. But giving of oneself and losing oneself are not the same thing. Losing oneself stems from weakness, while giving comes from a place of strength or love.

Let's go back to Lisa. Simon wanted her to compromise her career choices, for no real reason. But this would have been detrimental to her core self. She would have resented him in the future, and he probably would have continued to push her to compromise her self-esteem and values in other ways. Healthy compromise, on the other hand, comes from a place of strength or love. For example, if Lisa and Simon were planning to live in a third-world country, where it's not easy to find a position in special ed, they could discuss, as two adults, how to resolve the situation. If she said, "Although I have always wanted to be a special-ed teacher, my desire to marry you is stronger, and if it means that I have to change professions, I am ready to do that," that would have been an expression of her strong self. The compromise would have been real giving, as long as it was a conscious choice and not something she was pushed into.

Healthy compromise doesn't compromise oneself. It is an expression of strong self-esteem. The result of healthy compromise is a healthier sense of self.

Situation #2:
"Why do I keep going back to this guy when I know that he's not good for me?"

A woman named Rebecca came to see me about a problem she was having breaking off a relationship. She explained:

> Someone introduced me to Mark. I knew right away that there wasn't a future for us, although we always spoke about marriage. I never respected him, and I could never see him as part of my life. Nonetheless, it was hard for me to break away. Mark was so charismatic and exciting, I was afraid that I would be bored with a healthy, normal guy. We dated for a while and enjoyed each other's company, but I knew that he wasn't good for me. I finally got up the strength to break it off. But a few days later, we ran into each other…and we decided to give our relationship another chance. I was thrilled for about a week, and then I started to remember how bad Mark was for me. His lack of purpose and productivity in life always pulled me off course. It took me a couple of weeks to get fed up and break up again. We went back and forth four times. We're no longer seeing each other, but I still think about him, and I'm afraid that if I see Mark again I'll slip back into dating him again.

No one likes to feel out of control. If you find yourself going against your rational impulses and healthy convictions, it may be a sign that your boundaries need strengthening. You have to learn when to say no. You also have to learn to respect your needs and hold onto your convictions to do the right thing.

When you uphold your boundaries, you feel good about your-self; when you stick to your guns, it bolsters your self-esteem. It's a positive cycle: the higher your self-esteem, the more comfortable you'll be in establishing and maintaining boundaries.

Breaking Up

If you're trying to break out of a relationship that's not good for you, follow the steps below.

1. First create a motto, for example: "I want to be in a relationship that's healthy and respectable." Define what you think a healthy and respectable relationship is. For example, you might say, it's when you feel good about yourself, respect the man you're dating, and feel that the relationship is helping you become your best self.

2. List all the reasons why this man could not be a potential mate and why the relationship isn't working. *Be careful to articulate all of the issues.*

3. Clarify and affirm the following: "I am capable of controlling my choices and thoughts, which will ultimately give me control over my feelings. It might not be easy, but I can do it!" (We all have the ability to control our choices. Unfortunately, we only utilize this potential to a small degree. We will further discuss the power of our ability to choose in chapter 11.)

4. Plan out how you're going to break up and include any obstacles that you may encounter. For example, you might write: "When I break up, I will be clear and firm. I have to be careful not to let him throw me off. If he does, I will say _____ (fill in the blank)." It may help to rehearse your game plan with a friend.

5. After writing all of this down, keep it in a place that's very accessible.

6. Create a support team of friends and/or family who can (and want to) help you stay strong, so that you can call them if you have a weak moment.

Staying Away
Breaking up is half the battle. Staying away is the other half.

1. Read over all of the reasons your "ex" wasn't a good match for you, especially if you're having a weak moment.

2. Create a "stay away" motto. For instance: "Since I am capable of controlling my choices and feelings, I will exercise this power. This includes choosing to *not* recall his positive aspects, especially because those rose-colored memories can weaken my resolve to stay away." (Isn't it strange that after the breakup all you can think about are his good points?)

3. Get rid of or put away all mementos. (This might sound extreme, but if the desire to go back to a bad relationship is very strong, this step is a necessity.)

4. Stay in close contact with your support team. Call them the second you have a weak moment.

I sat down with Rebecca and we went over these steps. She clarified the fact that she indeed needed to be in a relationship with someone she respected. She created a vision of what that man might be like. She believed in her ability to control her choices. She wrote it all down clearly, including a clear description of all of his bad points. She was strong for about six months, and then she came to me, very upset with herself. She said, "I don't know what happened to me! Yesterday, I knew that Mark was no good for me. I was totally clear. Today, I found myself writing him an email. What happened to me?"

Okay, so she had a fall. It happens. The good news is that you can make that fall work for you if you turn it into increased conviction. Increased conviction sounds like this: "That's it! I am not going to make the same mistake. I have to review and strengthen the reasons I broke up! I have to stop myself from recalling his good points. I have a support team. Next time, I will call one of the people on the team and not the man I was dating."

Rebecca did strengthen herself. She got back up but this time she was stronger and clearer. After that, she never went back to Mark again. She met her future husband about a year later. When she told me about him, she said, "I can't believe I feel this way about a healthy, productive guy. I never thought it would happen! He's so responsible, fun, interesting, intelligent, motivated, attractive… He's a breath of fresh air." Once Rebecca strengthened herself, her boundaries, and her definition of what she needed, she was truly able to empty her cup (of the wrong relationship) and make the final break.

Another woman named Denise had a similar problem. Denise, like Rebecca, had been dating a guy that she knew she couldn't build a life with, and she was having trouble breaking up with him. She came to see me and explained the problem: Rob was often depressed and had a hard time communicating. He had a habit of jumping from job to job. Denise, on the other hand, had a full-time position she was committed to. She had also spent a lot of time creating life goals that she wanted to accomplish. Rob wasn't interested in change; he was happily plodding his way through life without any ambition. And yet, despite all of this, Denise was still enamored of Rob. She was very taken by his looks, and he also treated her very well. She felt paralyzed by her mixed feelings.

Denise's confusion pushed her to investigate her intense need for love and approval. Her need for these things was blocking her real dream of building a life with a man who wanted similar things. She started to understand that her feelings for Rob weren't based on real love after all, just a neediness and comfortable security. She realized that what she longed for was real love, which would be freeing, nurturing, and growth oriented. Yet even with this newfound awareness, she didn't stop dating him, because she was afraid she'd never find anyone else (an all-too-common theme). Denise and I worked through the breakup and stay-away steps listed above, and finally she found the strength. She realized that even if she didn't find anyone else, dating this man was draining her of her vitality, and marrying him would be even worse.

Denise broke it off and began dating other men. The only problem then was that every man she met, she compared to Rob. No one was as attractive to her as he was. I advised her that she needed to let go of that experience and, instead, imagine dating a man with similar life goals to her – someone she could respect and appreciate. She should obviously be attracted to him, but perhaps the attraction didn't need to be as intense and all-encompassing.

A short while later, Denise met a man just like she had imagined. She called to tell me about him, and how he was someone she truly respected and cared about. Besides that, he really liked her. She said that even though the attraction didn't bowl her over, it was definitely there. As her feelings for him grew, her attraction became stronger, and at the same time she realized that there was so much more to their relationship than attraction. After they got married, she understood for the first time in her life that love was not the same thing as neediness. Once she committed herself to finding a man with whom she could build a healthy relationship, she was able to step out of the doomed relationship she was in.

Situation #3:
"Who is he dating, his mother or me?"

First of all, why is everyone always complaining about mothers-in-law? What about fathers-in-law? It seems that most of the time, it is the mother-in-law in particular who is perceived as creating problems. To be fair, it's rarely her fault alone. The worst situations erupt when you combine an overbearing mother with a mama's boy who has a hard time standing up for himself. If you're the number two woman in a man's life, after his mother, consider it a red flag.

The in-law issue has been so prevalent throughout time that even the Bible mentions it. At the beginning of the book of Genesis, there is a directive: "Therefore a man shall leave his father and his mother and cleave to his wife, and they shall become one flesh."[12] The same directive ultimately applies to a woman as well. Obviously the Bible is not suggesting that you ignore your parents when you get married. But it is giving a clear message: Be careful with your allegiances. Your spouse is your priority; he/she comes first. And although it is more common for a man to be confused regarding his allegiance to his spouse versus mother, women are not immune to this problem. A woman has to make sure that she is setting appropriate boundaries with her mother and father as well. Of course she should maintain her close relationship with her parents, but her husband must know that he is number one in her life.

It is important to keep this in mind while dating because once you are married, your allegiances to each other might be tested. (Although some couples don't struggle with in-law issues, many do.) For example, some in-laws have a tendency to

---

12. Genesis 2:24.

undermine their child's marriage by bad-mouthing their son-in-law or daughter-in-law to their child. In order to avoid this or other destructive tendencies, it is important for the couple to create a strong, united front. By doing so, you should make it clear to both sets of parents that you will not tolerate them bad-mouthing your spouse to you, or bad-mouthing you to your spouse (whether your spouse is present or not). If your parents are well meaning and they have constructive criticism, which should be infrequent, they can sit down with both of you and have an open, positive discussion. (If it is a sensitive issue, they can speak to one of the spouses, as long as it is respectful and constructive.)

In order to create this united front once married, you want to make sure (before marriage) that the man you're dating has his allegiances clear. If the couple is successful in creating a united front and establishing healthy boundaries with their in-laws, they will have built a foundation that will not be easily undermined. Once this foundation is in place, they will be better able to build a positive and productive relationship with their in-laws.

Truth be told, it is not easy for a mother to let go of her son. Her relationship with him will and should change to a certain degree after he marries. But that is the challenge of this stage in life. There are some very special women who *are* able to manage it gracefully; they really should be applauded.

Situation #4:
"I keep getting into these codependent relationships."

There are many misconceptions as to what a codependent relationship is. Any close relationship – with friends, relatives, or your spouse – requires some level of healthy dependence. You are there for each other, you help each other out in various ways. There would be no trust if you couldn't depend on the other person to a certain extent, and vice versa. A codependent relationship, however, goes beyond the normal level of dependence. It's when two people actually depend on each other for dear life. Neither feel that they can stand on their own two feet; they rely on each other for their sense of worthiness and often for their sense of identity. They can only love themselves through the other person's eyes. Their boundaries are obviously not well defined and since "two can be one only if one can be two" (see page 46 for explanation), they have no real potential for genuine closeness.

I was approached by a woman named Pamela regarding Dave, a man she had been dating for a while. Although they had spoken about marriage, she had serious doubts that it would ever happen. She was having trouble respecting Dave. Even though he was smart, he never pushed himself to attend college because he lacked initiative and direction. And because he never worked on his character, he had the emotional maturity of a much younger man. Pamela was the opposite: she had finished college and had taken time to work on herself. Even though she said she loved him, she was sick of nagging and mothering him. I supported her in moving forward.

A few days later, I saw Pamela and asked her what had happened with Dave. She said, "I broke it off, but then we got back

together. He just can't survive without me! I can't do this to him."
In reality, she also couldn't survive without him. Or better said,
she couldn't survive without him needing her. Her whole sense
of self and value was based on him needing her. Dave needed
her for his self-definition and Pamela needed him for hers. Both
sides of a codependent relationship are really screaming out, "I
don't have a self without you!" or, "I don't know who I am without you!" That's why they're holding on for dear life.

I told Pamela that if she wanted to stay together and build
a healthy relationship with Dave, they would first need to take a
break. During that separation, Dave needed to seek counseling
from people who could really help him, instead of leaning on
Pamela. She, simultaneously, needed to develop her own self-
esteem and self-definition, instead of depending on his neediness to feel a sense of worth. If they stayed together without
doing this work, they would simply be using each other, and
chances are that neither would ever grow up.

The paradigm of a codependent relationship is that one
partner is weak, while the other is strong, as in the case of
Pamela and Dave. The gridlock of a codependent relationship
is the result of the strong person needing the weak person to
be weak...and simultaneously, the weak person needing the
strong person to be strong. This is the dance of codependence.
If the weak person suddenly becomes empowered, it throws
the dance off and the dancers are then out of sync. Since the
codependent dance does not work in solo, each partner does
his or her best to keep the other stuck in the codependence;
hence the gridlock.

The "I can't live without you" connection that Dave and
Pamela felt was actually what psychologists call "enmeshment,"
the loss of one's self into another person. Many people confuse

closeness with enmeshment. A parent can be enmeshed with a child, a friend can be enmeshed with a friend, and of course, a woman can be enmeshed with the man she's dating, or vice versa. With enmeshment your personal identity blurs into the identity of the other person. You might even start to think and feel as if you are the other person. An enmeshed relationship looks something like this:

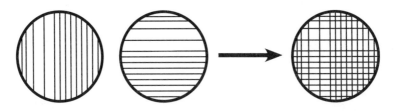

The couple has lost their individual identities in one another — the transition from separate to one happened too quickly, suddenly, and effortlessly.

Although *not* every enmeshed relationship is codependent, every codependent relationship *is* enmeshed. It is possible for one side of a relationship to be enmeshed. If both sides are enmeshed, the relationship is typically codependent. For example, if the situation with Pamela and Dave were different, if Pamela had been a healthy, strong woman and Dave lost his identity in the relationship (and she was upset about it, rather than empowered by it), this would have been a situation of one-sided enmeshment, not codependence.

Love, on the other hand, is not a loss of self in another. Love is a voluntary, mature giving of self to another, as opposed to an obsessive, needy type of giving. It is not trying to be the other. Rather, it is being oneself and accepting the other, realistically, with his or her flaws and differences. In a loving relationship, each wants the other to be maximized. Each takes joy in the other's success. Neither person desires to see the other as weak, limited, or broken.

Take the example of Brian, a man on his second marriage. Although Brian had children from his first marriage, his second wife, also on her second marriage, did not. When their first child was born, Brian was thrilled to be a father. But what really moved him was seeing his wife's joy upon experiencing being a mother for the first time.

The diagram of a loving relationship looks something like this:

With love, the circles breathe. They get very close, but they can also distance themselves. Every married couple experiences cycles of more intense closeness verses times of less intense closeness. At times, the circles completely coincide. There is a profound closeness and oneness formed as the two give themselves and give of themselves. But they are not holding on for dear life. They each have a life – and they are giving of their life! That's why some say that in a loving relationship, 1+1=100. When two people pool their strengths, their wisdom, and their energy, the whole is greater than the sum of its parts.

In a healthy relationship, there is constant give and take. Both give, both receive. Of course, there are times in a healthy relationship when one is more needy and therefore more of a receiver. But this is very different from the strong-versus-weak dance of codependence. The codependent couple need to realize that until they each develop their separate identities, their individual sense of worthiness, and seek ways to heal themselves, they will never taste the joy of true love. As they establish healthy boundaries in their lives, they'll open the door to healthy dating possibilities.

The sign of a balanced relationship is that it doesn't throw your entire life into turmoil. A healthy relationship enables both parties to maximize their potential. Just make sure that you take it slow. If you feel like you're falling into the other person, it's not a good sign. People should consciously merge together, through maturely sharing, opening up, and letting the other person into their worlds.

Situation #5:
"I feel like a magnet for abusive men."

It is difficult for me to include this section on abusive men in my book, because I have had the good fortune of meeting and working with so many wonderful men. When reading this section, it is important to remember that most men do not fall into this category. I say this because some women have a tendency to be paranoid about this issue, to the extent that any show of anger is already taken to be "abusive." This being said, there are some harmful men walking around out there, and it's essential to know how to spot them.

Signs of an Abusive Relationship

Here are a few of the most common warning signs to help you uncover abusive tendencies. You'll notice that most of these signs are essentially boundary violations.

1. Does he push your boundaries, your limits?
2. Is he very moody (does he have big mood swings)? Is he very nice to you one day, mean and obnoxious the next?
3. Does he tell you who to be friends with? Is he rude and/or insulting to your friends?
4. Does he criticize your appearance (the clothes you wear, your hairstyle, etc.)?
5. How does he react in situations of frustration: waiting for the waiter, traffic jams, waiting for you to get ready?
6. Does he speak to you in a disrespectful or hurtful way?
7. Has he threatened to hurt you or your family members?
8. Does he take responsibility for his actions? Does he, instead, blame everyone else (mother, boss, YOU)?
9. Is he very jealous and/or possessive (checking up on who you called, who's calling you; does he read your e-mails/texts)?
10. Do you often find yourself alienated suddenly from friends and family, since you've been dating him?

The scope of this book isn't broad enough to address the type of serious boundaries that are broken in abusive relationships. If you're in a relationship that is even touched by abuse, the best solution is to seek counseling from an experienced professional. Anyone who feels that she might be in trouble should seek assistance from the National Domestic Violence Hotline at 1-800-799-7233.

Tying It All Together

When you're dating, boundaries can be crucial because they surround, define, and protect you. They also help you clarify and maintain your convictions. Boundaries protect your relationship from becoming unhealthy; they allow you to be close to someone, but not lost in them. King Solomon, an ancient Jewish king who was renowned for his wisdom, summed boundaries up beautifully when he wrote, "He who can't rule his own spirit is like a city that is broken down and without walls."[13]

A person needs walls, or boundaries, in life. Internal boundaries are essential for self-control. For example, to gain the strength to break up with someone who's not right for you, you need to remind yourself of all the negative repercussions of the relationship. In this way you build healthy walls, which allow you to stick to your inner convictions. Boundaries are also essential for protection from the outside, from destructive people. A boundary, in this sense, is like a wall that guards one's *self*. When your boundaries are in place, you'll be able to consciously allow yourself to be vulnerable. This will open the doors to the merging and blending of the unified oneness of a healthy marriage.

13. Proverbs 25:28.

QUESTION #5:

What do people you are close to have to say about the person you are dating?

*W*hat is the general feedback that you are receiving from people close to you? If they volunteer their opinions, listen carefully. One of your friends might not hit it off with the man or woman you are dating or might not even like him or her. But that shouldn't be a warning sign. There is no one in this world who is liked by everyone. However, if *everyone* (or almost everyone) *that you trust* is telling you that something is wrong, take it seriously.

Often, when I lecture on this topic, people approach me and tell me that they've made terrible mistakes because they never asked themselves this question. During one of my classes, a woman raised her hand and said, "I wish I had heard this advice a few years ago. When I was dating my now ex-husband, everyone that I am close to told me that I was making a mistake. I didn't listen."

As soon as she finished sharing her experience, another woman raised her hand and said, "Same here. I'm divorced with children. Everyone I knew told me that my ex-husband was, and still is, immature and incompetent. But I didn't listen… I thought that I knew better."

I've heard these confessions all too often. On the one hand, you want to trust yourself, to listen to your inner voice. But you have to remember that those "elements of infatuation" are doing a number on you. Infatuation feels good and you don't want to let that feeling go. And those feelings can lure you into situations you may regret for the rest of your life.

Infatuation is so powerful that it can even do damage on the subconscious level. For example, a woman named Brenda once told me a story about a man she had dated. Although he was rude and inconsiderate, she couldn't stop thinking about him. She was so attracted to him that she didn't want to admit the truth: he had the maturity of a 16-year-old. She was so worried that her friends and family would see through him that she never introduced him to them. But it wasn't a conscious decision. She didn't sit down one day and decide, "I am not introducing the man I am dating to my family and friends." It was an unconscious decision. She didn't fully realize that she was avoiding introducing them until they started suspiciously questioning her.

If you want to learn to trust your inner voice, you have to learn to pay attention. You have to realize that your eyes are partially closed. To run a reality check on your relationship, be open to hearing what other people are telling you. Remember, their eyes are not partially closed or blinded by infatuation; yours may be. Pay attention to what people you *trust* think. If you trust a person and know that he or she is looking out for your good, there is no reason to be defensive. If you're feeling defensive, figure out why – there's a chance you might be in denial.

How Do You Gauge the Responses
of People That You Trust?

It is entirely possible that someone or a few people won't "get" the person you are dating. But if it's just an issue of personal taste, they'll usually say something like, "I wouldn't have imagined you with someone like him/her," or, "Are you sure that he/she's not too quiet for you?" Those statements have a different tone and charge than, "I get a really bad vibe from this guy. He doesn't seem right for you at all," or, "I'm really worried about your future. I think you're making a big mistake." When people are scared for us, chances are they're tuning in to a real problem.

Keep in mind that sometimes friends have suspicions that something is wrong, but they keep their suspicions to themselves. Maybe it's because they have a hard time with confrontation and/or they're uncomfortable approaching you. Sometimes, it's because they don't fully trust their own perceptions. Maybe they think that you'll be defensive and won't listen anyway, so why bother. Whatever the case, it's *very* common, after a breakup or divorce, for someone's friends to say something like, "I knew you were going to have a hard time with him... I never liked him from the beginning." Or, "I'm not surprised things didn't work out. Something about him made me nervous." It is essential that you let your friends know, when you're dating, that you are open to their feedback.

Take, for example, Fran, a typically happy bride-to-be planning her wedding. Throughout the engagement period, her fiancé was being mildly flirtatious with a few of her close friends. He would call each one, separately, to discuss wedding details. At first, it was very "innocent." However, as the phone calls continued, he tried to get more and more personal and spoke less and less about wedding arrangements. Each friend became increasingly uncomfortable about his phone calls but never spoke up because they were afraid to rock the boat. They also thought that Fran would get defensive and angry. Finally, one girlfriend told Fran about the phone calls, but it was two days before the wedding! As soon as she expressed her reservations about the groom, the others confessed they had also witnessed inappropriate behavior. The wedding was called off literally at the last minute.

When you're dating someone, it's important to ask your friends directly what they think. Let them know that your ears are open, even if your eyes might be a bit out of focus. I am not suggesting that you have to take a poll. But what you can do is ask them questions, such as:

* You haven't given me any feedback about the person I am dating. I'm really interested in your opinion.
* You're usually pretty talkative and opinionated. Is there a reason that you're being so quiet about the person I'm dating? I'm open to hearing your feedback about him/her.

Or simply,

* So, what do you think about him/her?

Besides asking your friends these important questions, there's another way to avoid getting burned like Fran did. Any and every time you get fooled into falling for the wrong man or woman, write about how it happened and what the red flags were that you missed. If you don't write about your feelings when they're fresh, you'll miss the opportunity to learn from your mistakes.

Questions to Ask Yourself After a Relationship Fails

The most profound wisdom we have is what we've learned from our errors, and yes, we're all human and we all make mistakes. Asking yourself these questions should help:

1. How did I justify my behavior?
2. How did I justify his/her behavior?
3. Could I hear that inner voice warning me that something was wrong?
4. Did I consciously ignore that inner voice?
5. What am I going to do differently next time? How am I going to make sure that I remember this insight?

The more you investigate your behavior, the better you'll be able to prevent future heartache. The wisdom you gain is well worth the effort.

CHAPTER SIX

QUESTION #6:

Do you respect the person you are dating?
Is there mutual respect?

*Y*ou might be thinking, if I didn't respect the person I was dating, why in the world would I be with him or her? As we discussed in the introduction, you can have chemistry with people you *don't even like* – so you can certainly have chemistry with people you don't respect! It all comes back to infatuation.

There is a difference between respect and what I call "puppy admiration": when infatuated, people tend to look at each other with all-adoring, "he's so amazing" eyes. True respect means accepting someone and honoring his or her thoughts and feelings. Puppy admiration, on the other hand, magnifies a couple of good traits or talents in one's "object of infatuation," and completely blocks out the negative. This tunnel vision can convince you that the person you're dating is perfect for you. The trickiest part of puppy admiration is that it feels like respect; indeed you seem to be looking up to this person. But, in reality, it's an illusion.

The essential meaning of the word "respect" is "to look at," from the Latin *respicere*, meaning just that. We can only respect a person if we are "looking at" and relating to who he or she is. Infatuation blocks our ability to truly see this. Without true

"vision," which includes a realistic understanding of how different this person might be from us, respect is impossible. The
difference between puppy admiration and respect is that when
we respect someone, we see and appreciate his or her uniqueness. The ability to do this increases in marriage, if both partners
choose to focus on the benefits of their differences. This is one
of the essential signs of a mature marriage: the acceptance and
appreciation of a couple's differences.

Warning: In chapter 1, I stressed how important it is to
share values and goals. When I use the word *differences* here, I
refer to personality differences, not value differences. Besides
this, keep in mind that I am not suggesting that you go out
and look for the person who is most different from you. On
the contrary, you want to look for similarities. Don't worry,
the differences will be there; at the very least there will be gender differences to deal with. However, when viewed correctly,
these differences become important building blocks toward a
profound marriage.

Is it possible to be too similar? Yes. Usually, when a couple
are too similar, they feel that the relationship gets stuck. A
couple of common complaints I have heard from dating couples
who are too similar are:

* "This is ridiculous! We both need someone to
  draw us out of ourselves. We are both somewhat
  introverted. This isn't going anywhere."

* "I know that I get emotional....but so does he. I
  tend to dramatize, but I think he's even worse.
  There's way too much emotional energy here. I
  don't know if we would survive a marriage but
  one thing is for sure: even if we did, our children
  would not!"

I think that the point is clear. Similarities CAN get in the way. Therefore, a couple should check that their values match up, that the differences they perceive in each other are not too great and that their similarities create symmetry, not nausea.

Check Your Respect Quotient

Not sure if you really respect the person you're dating? Ask yourself the following questions:

1. Can I see that the person I am dating is different from me? If so, how?
2. List the benefits of marrying a person who has these traits.
3. What are the strengths of the person I am dating? Do I appreciate them?
4. What are his or her weaknesses? Can I respect and accept him or her with these weaknesses?
5. What are his or her values? Do I respect and appreciate them?
6. What are his or her goals? Do I respect and appreciate them?
7. What are his or her interests? Do I respect and appreciate them?
8. The person I am dating inspires me to be more
_____.

Now flip the questions around and ask them about yourself. For example: "Does he or she recognize and respect my values? Can he or she see how I am different from him/her? Does he/she see the benefits to these differences?"

You need to make sure that there's *mutual respect*.

Quite often, people in the grip of infatuation might not pay attention to blatant signs that the person they're dating doesn't respect them. A number of women have told me that men they've dated, who might be better educated or smarter in some ways, have said things like, "Oh, you wouldn't understand this article. It's above your head." Or, "Why are you so interested in my thesis? You don't know a thing about politics." They put up with these statements because they were so attracted to the men they were dating. They didn't want to face the facts, until the statements became intolerable. Likewise, many men have shared with me their pain and frustration when women have said things like, "That restaurant is probably too pricey for a guy like you." Or, "You probably would never confront someone about a poorly done job –you're too 'nice.'"

Some might argue that true respect – respect that is tried and tested – only develops after years of commitment in marriage. They argue that it takes years of work to accept the other person's separateness, learning to love him or her all the same. Although this may be true, there must be a basis for respect right from the beginning.

Welcome to the "Gap"

There are certain gaps that can threaten the respect in a relationship. For example, if there is a big educational gap, you have to be careful. If the woman is more educated, she has to be especially careful. When a woman feels like she's smarter than the man she is with, she tends to step all over him. I have seen this so often that I could probably write a book on this subject alone.

I remember a particular couple where the woman, Arlene, was smarter, sharper, and more educated than the man she was dating. I warned her about this, but the infatuation was so great that she didn't want to hear it. She insisted that his other qualities were more important. As she tried to convince me, I could tell that she was trying to convince herself as well. After they married, Arlene slowly began to badger her husband with endless insults. She was annoyed that he wasn't as ambitious as she was. She was bothered by the fact that her paycheck was twice the size of his. Arlene knew that she would be making double his salary when she first met him. The only thing that changed was that when the infatuation wore off, her eyes were opened. Unfortunately, she continued to harass him with insults, and they eventually suffered a bitter divorce.

(I should add that I have seen women who are smarter than their husbands and don't step all over them. These are exceptional women. However, in all cases, these women are still able to respect their husbands for traits other than intelligence.)

A large age gap is another potential red flag. In my experience, if the man is up to ten years older, it's usually not a problem (unless he is vastly more educated or worldly). But after ten years, you have to be more cautious. A husband and wife must feel like equals in order to have a healthy relationship. Obviously, if he is way beyond her in life experience and maturity, he might look down on her.

I would like to share an insight from ancient Jewish philosophy that sheds some light on this subject. There is a saying: "Make for yourself a mentor [or teacher, '*Rav*' in Hebrew]; acquire a friend for yourself; and be sure to judge everyone favorably" (Ethics of the Fathers, 1:6).

Besides being a source of good advice, these words also teach us about three different types of relationships everyone should have in his or her life:

1. **Mentors:** These are people who are ahead of us in life. They are wiser and more experienced. We need to seek out mentors and learn how to be guided by them.

2. **Friends or peers:** These people are our equals. They tend to be at similar stages in life to ours. Sometimes we cry on their shoulders, sometimes they cry on our shoulders. We confide in them and they confide in us. It is an equal relationship.

3. **Mentorees:** In the third category, we are the mentors; others are guided by us. Of course we need to judge everyone favorably, but especially our mentorees. They are less experienced and less wise than we are, and they will definitely make mistakes that we would never make.

A husband and wife should fit into the second category. Although a woman naturally wants to look up to her husband, he still needs to be in the realm of "peer." The couple must, therefore, relate to each other as equals. If he is much older, this equal friendship might not exist. For example, if a woman marries her teacher or professor, she initially may be awed by his knowledge. But sooner or later she's going to feel that she just doesn't measure up. That being said, there certainly are couples who have a fifteen-year age gap and yet it works in a healthy way – but it only works if they relate to each other as peers and not as father-daughter.

What if she's the one who's older? It depends on how mature the man is. If she's a year or two older, the difference might not be noticed. If she is four or five years older, he would have to be extraordinarily mature in order to be a healthy partner for marriage. (I have seen quite of few of these marriages work.) Otherwise, guess who's playing Mommy? Ultimately, the couple must ask themselves: Is there mutual respect? Does she really respect him? If not, they might end up mistreating each other.

A large "social class" gap can also threaten a relationship. I once spoke with Elissa, a woman who illustrated this point clearly. She confessed that she had trouble dating guys who weren't wealthy because she couldn't respect them. She sincerely wished that she could date a great guy "without big money." As our conversation progressed, she finally realized what the real problem was: she didn't want to repeat her parents' marriage.

Her mother came from a rich family. Her father came from a poor home. Although Elissa grew up wealthy (due to her mother's inheritance), she was always aware that her mother never respected her father. Because he maintained his old mentality and manners, he was always "poor" in his wife's eyes. As a result, she saw her mother routinely step all over him. Elissa, who was now in her late 20s, was terrified of making the same mistake. And she should be!

Are there people from upper-class families who are happily married to people from lower-class families? Of course. But it does take a lot of work, and not everyone is prepared to do this kind of work. If you're considering a spouse from a different social class, you must do some sober thinking. Sober thinking means seeing beyond the infatuation and looking at the respect factor. Start by asking yourself the following questions:

- * Are you both ready to break out of your mentalities?
- * Are you willing to put up with different habits?
- * Can you both agree on how you define a "luxury" versus a "necessity"?

Social class differences can also play out on a smaller scale, such as a difference in table manners. But these seemingly insignificant habits can be destructive. In the year 2005, a fascinating study was conducted, funded by the U.S. government's National Institute of Child Health and Human Development. The study looked at the phenomenon of being irked by one's spouse's "disgusting" or uncouth habits. Some people call this phenomenon "social allergies." The research shows that these "allergies" can lead to divorce.[14] In the early stages of a relationship, a person might dismiss a habit as unimportant or even cute. For example, if someone tends to eat fast and sloppily due to being "so busy doing important things," this could be looked at with adoring eyes. But, once the infatuation wears off, the habit could become grating.

One of the key ingredients in a healthy and happy marriage is mutual respect. You both need it, you both deserve it. So it pays to take the time and energy to take a good look and make sure that it's there.

---

14. Michael R. Cunningham, Stephen R. Shamblen, Anita P. Barbee, and Lara K. Ault, "Social Allergies in Romantic Relationships: Behavioral Repetition, Emotional Sensitization, and Dissatisfaction in Dating Couples," *Personal Relationships* 12, no. 2 (June 2005): 273–95.

CHAPTER SEVEN

QUESTION #7:

Can you be open and honest with the person you are dating? Do you trust him or her?

*N*ina had been dating Joe for a while and was feeling very confused. She came to speak with me and explained why. "It's never been hard for me to open up and share my feelings. But as hard as I try, I just can't open up to Joe." As we spoke, Nina eventually admitted: "You know what? I just don't trust him! But we have such great chemistry. How is it possible to have such great chemistry with someone, yet not trust him?"

It's a good question. Having chemistry with someone doesn't mean that you can be emotionally intimate. In other words, physical chemistry and emotional intimacy are not the same thing. What is intimacy? It is commonly said that the word itself spells out its true meaning: *into-me-see* (intimacy). Emotional intimacy is letting a person in, allowing him or her to see…into your inner world, your thoughts, feelings, dreams, hopes, fears, insecurities, and experiences. Intimacy is sharing your true self with another person…and experiencing the sharing of his or her true self. According to the Merriam Webster's Collegiate Dictionary, *intimate* means "belonging to or characterizing one's deepest nature, intrinsic or essential, personal and closely associated, marked by a warm friendship through long association." Clearly, this type of experience doesn't happen without some conscious effort, and certainly not all at once. Emotional intimacy is an experience that is consciously nurtured and developed.

When Nina admitted that she had a hard time trusting Joe, she was actually revealing one of the most important truths about emotional intimacy: it can only exist if it's built on *trust*. Trust is the bedrock of intimacy; it's the ability to rely on someone because you believe that he or she has your best interests at heart. Although there are times in every relationship when people are insensitive to each other (we're all human), trust is based upon the belief and knowledge that these painful moments were not intentional.

Trust takes time to develop and flourishes when there is mutual commitment. But you *can* spot the potential for trust early in a relationship. It all comes back to the word "safe." You can start by taking the Trust Test.

Trust Test

1. Do I feel safe with the person I am dating? Can I let my guard down around him or her?
2. How does he treat people? How does he speak about others? Does he deride others?
3. Would I say that she is an honest person? Why?
4. Can I rely on him? To what extent?
5. What are my deepest, darkest secrets? Do I feel that she would eventually be able to handle these "secrets," accept me with them, and support me?

If you are satisfied with your answers to the Trust Test questions, you can feel confident that there's a basis for trust. Now it is safe to begin to open up, share some secrets and self-disclose. But first, let me clarify a few things about self-disclosure.

Three Secrets of Self-Disclosure

1. Self-disclosure doesn't mean that you spill out all of your dirty laundry. It also doesn't mean that you give a vivid history of all of the other people you've ever dated. Self-disclosure *does* mean that you can share incidents and secrets from your past that might affect your behavior and your relationship *in the present*. If you feel that you can't trust a person enough to eventually share this information, it's not a good sign. When people keep these types of secrets, it fosters alienation and loneliness, rather than emotional intimacy.

2. Be careful not to self-disclose prematurely! When you open up too quickly, you can scare people and/or put them on the defensive. You have to think about when, where, and how to open up. If you're not sure, speak to a friend or mentor who is in a healthy relationship.

3. Self-disclosure shouldn't be one-sided. Real emotional intimacy only develops if it's mutual, with each party putting out a card or two at a time. If one person is doing all of the opening up, it

could lead to an illusion of a close relationship. Although one person usually begins and takes the lead, ultimately, self-disclosure is safe only if it's reciprocated.

The Vulnerability Factor

Once we understand that emotional intimacy is based on trust, we can begin to understand the truth about vulnerability. Vulnerability is wonderful. It is an essential element in a close relationship. When you can finally let your guard down and reveal your struggles and imperfections, you can begin to experience a profound real-ness in your relationship. Only when you can take your "mask" off will you open the door to being loved for who you truly are, underneath the surface. This is what vulnerability is all about, and there's no doubt that it is a primary ingredient in a close relationship.

However, vulnerability also has a dark side. It is because of this dark side that so many people view vulnerability in a negative light. When is vulnerability a problem? When you fall into it…when you don't choose it. Vulnerability is a negative experience when you open up to someone you *don't trust*, when you open up prematurely or when you share too much too soon. These slip-ups happen to people who are infatuated and swept away with their emotions. That feeling of instant connection, which is rarely based on anything real, fools people into opening up more than they should. Often I hear people say, "I can't believe I opened up to him/her so quickly… What was I thinking?" Worse, this behavior often results in resentment, which can ruin a budding relationship.

The progression often looks like this:

INFATUATION

↓

FALSE SENSE OF EMOTIONAL INTIMACY

↓

PREMATURE DISCLOSURE

↓

PREMATURE VULNERABILITY

↓

HURT/REJECTION

↓

RESENTMENT

The goal is not to "fall into" vulnerability, but to choose it. Once you determine that your potential mate is trustworthy, then you can take steps towards letting your guard down and being vulnerable. It still takes a bit of courage, but it's not a blind risk. The truth is that only when you take those steps towards healthy vulnerability will you be able to build intimacy.

The positive cycle looks like this:

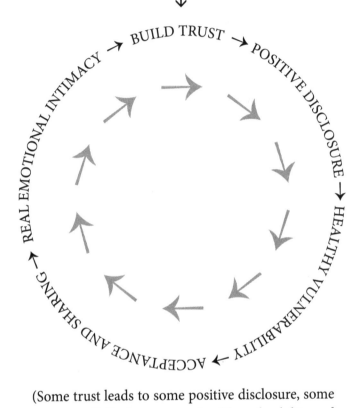

CONNECTION BASED ON SOMETHING REAL

(Some trust leads to some positive disclosure, some positive self-disclosure, some healthy vulerability, and some emotional intimacy, which in turn leads to more trust, more disclosure, etc.; the cycle keeps building)

This makes a lot of sense and sounds great...intellectually. The problem is internalizing this information emotionally. As much as people crave emotional intimacy, they also fear it. This fear is more common than we might think.

This was the case with Bruce, a man who once approached me about his relationship of six months. He really liked the girl he was dating, Dana, and felt that she was the one. On the one hand, he was excited about the prospect of marriage. On the other hand, he was scared. He was less afraid of commitment than scared of closeness. Bruce craved a close relationship, yet he always distanced himself from the woman he was dating just as things started taking off emotionally. There was always a "reason" for the distance: sometimes it was an argument (that he would typically start), sometimes he would get caught up in a work assignment (since he was a lawyer, it wasn't hard for him to lose himself in his job). Eventually, Bruce recognized his pattern of distancing himself, mostly due to the fact that Dana became increasingly frustrated with him. Luckily, he turned to one of his older married friends. Through their discussion he discovered that he suffered from a common *fear of emotional intimacy*. There are four common reasons a person might be afraid of intimacy. One of them, a fear of being swallowed up in a close relationship, is what Bruce struggled with.

Four Reasons for Fear of Emotional Intimacy

1. Fear of being swallowed up in a close relationship
2. Painful relationship experience in one's past
3. Insecurity and fear of rejection
4. Emotionally closed background and/or personality

So what happened to Bruce? His married friend instructed him, encouraged him, and served as a role model for healthy intimacy. Bruce observed how his married friend shared a closeness with his wife, yet maintained his own interests. He learned that closeness does not mean nullification of self. Bruce spent time establishing a more internal "self-concept." Although he was very confident and well defined in his professional life, his personal life needed some work. (It's very common for successful professionals to ignore their weakness in building relationships. It takes a lot of courage for people who are so successful in one sphere to face the sphere in which they lack development.) Bruce invested quality time developing his internal "self-concept" and simultaneously pushed himself to internalize the wonderful rewards of being in a close, nurturing marriage. As a result, he gained the strength to overcome his fears, and last I heard, he's very happily married to Dana.

Fear of Being Swallowed Up in a Close Relationship

Some people have a tendency to lose themselves or their identity in the person they're dating. If you equate closeness with loss of self, you might find yourself avoiding closeness at all cost. In order to overcome this particular fear, it is important to build personal boundaries and to create a vision of what it looks like to have a close relationship that nevertheless maintains healthy self-definition. As you strengthen your boundaries, your fear of getting swallowed up or smothered in a close relationship will lessen. (For more about boundaries and how to develop them, turn to chapter 4.)

Fear of emotional intimacy solution #1:
Build healthy personal boundaries to avoid loss of self.

Painful Relationship Experience in One's Past

A second reason for fear of intimacy is a painful relationship experience in one's past. This could be something a person went through personally or saw someone else go through. It could be anything from a dysfunctional relationship to losing a loved one. Whatever the case, these memories can create tremendous intimacy blocks in a person's life.

Jonathan once discussed with me his difficulty in sustaining relationships. His parents had a difficult marriage; they fought a lot and were constantly complaining about each other. He wondered why they didn't just get divorced. Eventually they did, but not before they exposed their son to years of negativity and hatred. When Jonathan came of age and his friends began dating, he preferred to spend his time playing computer games. They were safe and uncomplicated, unlike people. He was terrified of relationships and suppressed his need and desire to connect in a real way.

Jonathan hid behind his computer for a few years until he met Helene, a young woman who worked in his office. After chatting with him a few times, she realized where his tendency to avoid dating was stemming from. As he sensed that he could trust her, Jonathan pushed himself to open up, even though it was uncomfortable. Eventually, he started dating her. The fact that Helene was patient and nonjudgmental helped him take his initial shaky steps. Jonathan also invested time reading books about dating and marriage, which gave him various tools he was missing. He worked hard to discard the negative marriage images he had inherited from his parents' relationship. Jonathan and Helene eventually got married, and they have succeeded in building a fantastic, emotionally fulfilling relationship. Jonathan's role models for healthy emotional intimacy were Helene and the marriages he read about in his dating and marriage books.

The first step towards healthy intimacy is seeing and believing that it exists and that it is possible. Instead of falling in love with infatuation, you need to fall in love with true love, with emotional intimacy. If you cannot find real-life role models, you can look for role models in books.

The bottom line is that everyone is capable of creating emotional intimacy. And there's no better way to learn than through example. If you didn't see healthy intimacy growing up, it's never too late to seek out role models and learn from them.

The cliché "When there's a will there's a way" has a lot of truth to it.

Fear of emotional intimacy solution #2:
Seek role models of healthy emotional intimacy.

Insecurity and Fear of Rejection

A third cause of fear of intimacy is insecurity and fear of rejection. A very common worry is, "When the person I am dating sees who I really am, he'll run the other direction," or, "she'll get bored and drop me," etc. Many people are afraid to open up. As mentioned earlier, it does take some courage. The stronger your self-esteem, the easier it is to put yourself out there.

People are often unaware that they have a fear of rejection. This was the case with Jessica, who came to see me about her pattern in relationships. She would date a man until he was interested in her, but as soon as he started to like her, she would drop him. She felt bad about this tendency, and was starting to get a bad reputation. What Jessica came to understand was that underlying her behavior was a fear of emotional intimacy. She was afraid that if she were to seriously date, the man would quickly see through her or lose interest. Her behavior pattern was a camouflage for her insecurities.

Eventually Jessica was able to break her negative cycle and settle down with a wonderful man. She was only able to do this once she took some time out to build her self-esteem. She had to work hard but she's the first person to admit that every part of the struggle was worth it. (Her husband is the second.)

Self-esteem is a topic that deserves not only its own chapter, but its own book. I will not elaborate on this subject extensively. However, I will say a couple of essential things about this topic.

I once referred a girl named Lorraine to a therapist to help her develop self-esteem. This therapist didn't have any space for new clients, so she referred her to someone else. When this new therapist met Lorraine, she immediately asked her the most obvious question a therapist would ask, "Why are you in therapy? What do you want to work on?"

Lorraine answered, "I want to tackle my low self-esteem."

The therapist replied, "Oh, low self-esteem is just something you have to accept. It's a condition for life."

Lorraine was shocked. Had she not been struggling with her self-esteem, she would have stood up and walked out. What a ridiculous statement! Self-esteem is certainly something that can be built. A person needs the right guidance and a strong will in order to succeed. This guidance can be given by a coach, a therapist (a competent one), a healthy friend, or a good book.

If there's one thing that we have to believe in, it's our ability to change. This ability to change is what makes us profoundly human. In essence, you cannot change unless you believe that you can change. But you have to keep in mind that everyone has ups and downs in the growth process; that's normal. The path of growth is not a straight line – it has curves, swerves, and in short, turbulence. You just have to keep your eye on the goal and nurture yourself as you travel. As you make small strides in building your self-esteem, your fears of being accepted will lessen. Everyone without exception experiences rejection in life. The irony is that the more you can handle rejection, the less rejection you will tend to experience.

Fear of emotional intimacy solution #3:
Build self-esteem.

Emotionally Closed Background and/or Personality

A fourth cause for fear of intimacy is an emotionally closed background and/or personality. If you grew up in a home where there was very little affection or discussion of feelings, this could get in the way of forming a close intimate relationship in adulthood. In addition, if you tend to be shy or introverted, you might find yourself steering clear of intimacy.

Elaine struggled with this very issue. She was a refined, gentle woman who was on the shy side. She met a particular man whom she liked very much, and they dated for a while. Although they had a lot in common and enjoyed each other's company, he felt that she was too closed off. He complained about her lack of communication and responsiveness. Elaine was devastated. She had already envisioned herself marrying him. She tried to open up, but felt a tremendous block.

That relationship ended, but soon afterwards, she met a man who was even more wonderful in her eyes. They too hit it off and had a tremendous amount in common. However, after a few weeks he also began complaining about her lack of openness. At that point she called me to ask whether I thought she needed to go into therapy to work on her shyness. I told her that she had two choices: go for therapy in order to face her fears of opening up, or, push herself to open up, specifically about those fears.

Two days later Elaine called me, bursting with joy. She told me that although she was terrified to share her fears with the man she was dating, she forced herself and reaped immediate benefits. As Elaine told him about her fears of opening up, he reassured her that he would be patient and supportive; this in turn allowed her to open up even further. Elaine was really proud of herself. Soon after that they got engaged, and have built a very open and emotionally intimate marriage.

Sometimes you just have to dive in the deep end and push yourself to open up. It's best to practice with someone you trust. Even when you find someone to confide in, opening up can still be intimidating. The best way to practice is to write out what you want to say. Whether you're sharing your deepest secrets or your feelings about the person you're dating, you initially might want to open up through a letter or email, rather than verbally. Only through practice will you break through your initial fears.

The other half of opening up is learning how to listen. In addition to practicing communication, one also has to practice the art of listening. Many people list their spouses' "ability to listen" as the number-one reason they chose them. And as the saying goes, "When we are **s-i-l-e-n-t**...we can **l-i-s-t-e-n**." When you really listen to what someone else is saying, you give him or her a sense of sincere validation. Emotional intimacy is the mutual understanding and acceptance of each other. You can't develop this intimacy without being a good listener.

Fear of emotional intimacy solution #4:
Practice opening up.

Four Solutions to the
Fear of Emotional Intimacy
1. Develop clear personal boundaries and
self-identity.
2. Seek role models of healthy emotional
intimacy.
3. Build self-esteem.
4. Practice opening up.

The desire to be emotionally intimate with another special person is part of the human condition. Everybody is capable of creating emotional intimacy. All it takes is a strong will to experience it, some guidance from mentors and/or books, and a bit of courage to start opening up.

With Hindsight...

Over the years, I have met with many men and women about intimacy issues, and I have seen a recurring pattern.

Once people start to step out of their fears, once they start to experience true emotional intimacy, they commonly look back and say, "What was I so afraid of? What was I thinking?"

Once people step out of the false intimacy of infatuation and taste the real thing, they say something like, "That wasn't closeness... It was effortless, but it was insecure. When I was infatuated, there was always a part of me that didn't trust it. I was always nervous about it wearing off. But *this* is the real thing. I am fully present. Yes, I have to work for it, it doesn't 'just happen'…but it is real and profound."

The false intimacy of infatuation can be likened to junk food. It tastes great at the moment…but then it's gone (except for the calories, i.e., scars from a painful relationship). Real emotional intimacy is like a whole nourishing meal. Why cheat yourself?

CHAPTER EIGHT

QUESTION #8:

How well do you get along with the person you are dating? How is your communication?

I remember an eye-opening discussion I had with Roy, who once came to consult with me. When he told me that he was divorced, I asked him if he and his ex-wife argued a lot. I'll never forget his reply: "My ex-wife and I didn't even have one major disagreement." Two and a half years of marriage and no major arguments? I thought to myself, "Maybe if they had had it out, they would still be married." Sometimes people equate a good marriage with no arguing. What they don't realize is that when people squash and deny their negative feelings, they end up numbing their positive feelings as well. And they also build up resentment.

The truth is, a certain amount of arguing, when done right, can lead to great communication. Some arguing and disagreeing is normal and even healthy. The question, then, is *how much*? Also, if people fight often, why in the world do they continue dating? Let's explore the answers to these questions.

How much arguing and disagreeing is okay? Dr. John Gottman, author of *Why Marriages Succeed or Fail*, has done extensive research clarifying that there is a certain amount of negativity that any marriage can have and still be considered successful. According to Dr. Gottman, "Across the board we found there was a very specific ratio that exists between the amount of positivity and negativity in a stable marriage. That magic ratio is 5 to 1. In other words, as long as there is five times as much positive feeling and interaction between husband and wife as there is negative, we found the marriage was likely to be stable."[15] According to Dr. Gottman, it is preferable for the ratio not to drop under 20:1.[16] However, if the ratio is at least 5:1, the couple have the potential for building a happy marriage.

When couples exceed the healthy amount of arguing – when there is an overdose of confrontations – it's a troubling sign. Why do people pursue or stay in these types of relationships? If they can't get along before they marry, what makes them think they'll get along afterwards?

Here are four of the most common reasons dating couples stay together despite too much arguing:

1. First, infatuation may be covering up the fact that the two don't really like each other. The mutual attraction carries them both for a little while until suddenly their incompatibility and mutual dislike emerge and the negativity starts to flow. If they're lucky, at that point, they break up. However, if the infatuation is still intact, they tend to forget about

---

15. *Why Marriages Succeed or Fail* (New York: Fireside, 1994), p. 57.
16. Heard at the "Workshop on the Gottman Method," given to a group of professionals and educators by Dr. Toni Parker (one of Dr. Gottman's main disciples) on February 13, 2007, in Jerusalem.

the negative interactions and begin to date again. I know of a couple who went through this "break up–make up" cycle six times. They had very little in common; they annoyed each other to no end, and in general, didn't respect each other. Once broken up, they would again reminisce about the "good times" (the infatuation would kick in) and they would get back together…until the next fight. Finally, one of them realized that the relationship was futile and made the final break. Unfortunately, their mutual scars lasted quite some time.

2. A second reason people stay in these types of relationships is because they actually enjoy the adrenaline rush of a good fight. The term *dramaholics* was coined for these folks. The problem is that this drama becomes a substitute for real emotional intimacy. When there's a vacuum in the relationship, they subconsciously or semi-consciously fill it with the fire of fighting, which seems to keep their relationship alive. It might even be a conscious decision: some people will go so far as to say that they feel their relationship is dead if they don't frequently have a good fight. In truth, the fighting itself is killing the relationship; in addition to all of the pain it causes, it also prevents the pair from developing true communication.

3. There are couples who stay together amidst the arguing simply because they are used to each other. The comfort of familiarity can also be strengthened by the fear of finding someone new. People in

these types of relationships will actually say, "I'm comfortable with him/her." From the outside, this statement seems absurd! Comfortable? That's the last word anyone would use to describe their relationship, given all of the arguing. However, the fear that there's no one else out there keeps the couple stuck in this destructive cycle.

4. Denial is the fourth reason a couple might stay in this type of relationship. Even though there's an *unresolvable* issue in their relationship, they don't want to see or admit to it. A woman named Gail once told me about the man she almost married. Although she liked almost everything about Andrew, there was one thing that she couldn't swallow. He had a tendency to be slightly dishonest in business. Although it was minor, it went against her strongest value of honesty and integrity. That was her motto in life. She liked him so much that she tried not to pay attention to this blatant problem. However, every time she saw a hint of this dishonesty, she would withdraw from him and they would break up. After the breakup, Gail would begin to miss Andrew and ask herself if she was smart to give up on him when he had so many other good qualities. They would start dating again until his next "dishonesty" episode. This cycle continued until Gail realized that even though there was only one issue that she couldn't swallow, it was a *big* issue. It was huge enough to undermine her ability to trust Andrew, and she knew that without trust, there was no potential for a healthy marriage.

Four Reasons
Fighting Couples Stay Together
1. Infatuation covers up the fact that the two don't really like each other.
2. They are *dramaholics* — they actually enjoy the adrenaline rush of a good fight.
3. They are used to each other and are afraid to start over again with someone new.
4. Denial. They don't want to see the *unresolvable* issue in their relationship.

So what happens when the issue is *resolvable?* It can still lead to extensive arguing if the couple doesn't actively deal with it. It might be something as simple as how much time they should be spending together, or as serious as how to deal with the in-laws. Whatever the case, only when they sit down, learn to communicate, and set up a strategy to resolve the issue will the incessant fighting stop. It often happens that the couple become "locked into" a repetitive, destructive argument every time the issue comes up. In situations like this the assistance of a third, objective party might be the only way out of the gridlock.

The Importance of Communication

A major reason that couples argue too often is simply because they don't know how to communicate. Even though there may be no objective issues getting in their way, they can make a real mess of seemingly harmless conversations. Healthy dialogue is one of the most important elements in any relationship.

A man named Joel recently spoke with me about a communication problem he was having with Jen, the girl he was dating. When they met, they immediately hit it off and felt comfortable with each other. He was sure that he had met his future wife. However, a few weeks into the relationship, they began to argue and disagree. Upon analyzing his relationship, he clarified that they were well suited for each other: they shared goals and values, respected each other, and genuinely enjoyed each other's company. So, why all the fighting? The main thing getting in the way was that when it came to communication, Joel had more experience. Jen often fumbled her way through serious talks, saying the wrong things at the wrong times. They both decided to take action to fix the problem. They went together for a few sessions of premarital counseling. Jen picked up the necessary communication skills; Joel learned to be more patient with her, which boosted her self-confidence. I was overjoyed when he called me to tell me that he had proposed.

Communication is a vital tool for every healthy marriage and a huge subject in and of itself. Some people just need to learn some basic skills, through books or courses. Others need to spend time uprooting negative communication habits. It's essential for everyone to learn the methods for constructive arguing, since disagreements are bound to happen. Armed with the right information and tools, together with a strong will to create a loving marriage, you will succeed.

Once Married...

The key to avoiding destructive unhealthy arguing in marriage is – *no matter what, remember you are a team.* You can either argue to win, or argue to improve your relationship. If you are fighting with your spouse to win, you will end up turning him or her into your enemy. So in the end, no one wins.

There's an old Russian anecdote that expresses this idea beautifully: A man goes to his friend and says, "You know what? I bet you 1000 rubles that I can eat a pound of dirt!" His friend says, "Uch…you can't eat a pound of dirt. That's disgusting." The man says, "Yes, I can. I bet you 1000 rubles that I can." His friend says, "You've got a deal."

And so, this man brings over a pound of dirt in a bag and proceeds to eat the whole thing. His friend is amazed. The friend hands him 1000 rubles, then says to the man, "You know what? I bet you that I can also eat a pound of dirt." The man says, "You? No way!" His friend replies, "Yes, I can. I bet you 1000 rubles that I can!" The man answers him, "You've got a deal." His friend brings over a pound of dirt in a bag and eats the whole thing. The man then gives him 1000 rubles. A few minutes later, the man says to his friend, "You know what? I think that we both just ate a pound of dirt for free!"

If you don't want to "eat dirt" in your marriage, make your motto teamwork. Imagine watching a doubles' tennis match and suddenly one team begins to argue between themselves. In order to spite the other team member, one member decides to miss the ball instead of hitting it; then they both end up losing. You can't afford to forget that you're a team, which means that if something is bad for one of you, it's bad for both of you.

I know how difficult it is to think about these things when you are angry at your mate. One's primal instinct at that moment is to yell and scream and even to spite the person who is the most important to you. Therefore, it is essential to spend time contemplating and internalizing this truth. The most ideal time for this contemplation is when there is no friction in the marriage, when you are getting along well. This is also the best time to strategize with your spouse about how you're going to deal with conflict when it arises. You want to emphasize that the reason for arguing is to build, not to destroy.

Exercise:
A Team in Two Minutes

Try this exercise: Set aside two minutes a day (on the clock) and think about the two of you – you and your spouse – as a team. Think about how significant you are to one another. Focus on all of the wonderful talents and abilities of your mate or potential mate. Contemplate the fact that these attributes complement yours, and together, you are greater than the sum of your parts. Do this exercise regularly two minutes a day for one month. If you're consistent, you'll undoubtedly find yourself fighting and arguing less. You'll be able to deal with your frustration in a more mature, productive way.

Perhaps one of the most painful things to see is a couple who started out their marriage with hopes of creating a strong, loving relationship, and instead, tear each other apart. I know of a situation where a man was on a train minding his own business. He suddenly heard a couple fighting a few seats over. She said, "Where's our train ticket? You put it in your wallet. We're going to be thrown off the train if you don't find it." He said, "You put it in your purse." She said, "I didn't even bring my purse. You know that!" He said, "How do you expect me to remember every detail?" She yelled, "It's your fault!" He yelled back, "No, it's your fault!" By now, everyone was watching them have it out: it's your fault...no it's yours... Finally a man yelled, "You know what? It's my fault, blame me... Now stop fighting!" They stopped fighting for a few minutes, but then started up again until the conductor came around to collect the tickets. Luckily they found the ticket on the floor and that was the end of that. The couple forgot that they were on the same team. It's so clear to everyone on the outside that they're hurting themselves by hurting each other. If only they could see it themselves.

A good marriage is not one that's conflict free. It's normal for two people to disagree and argue at times. The question is, will these disagreements and arguments undermine your relationship, or will you learn to use them as building blocks towards a close, healthy marriage?

CHAPTER NINE

QUESTION #9:

Does the person you are dating bring out the best in you?

*I*t's very common to have chemistry with people who bring out the worst in you. The problem is that it's possible to get so caught up in "the feelings of infatuation" that you don't realize that the person you're dating is bringing out your unhealthy side.

Take, for example, Vanessa, a woman in her late 20s who grappled with various addictive tendencies. After she decided to pull her life together, she spent a good two years working on herself in therapy and at support groups. She was doing unbelievably well, had built up a tremendous amount of self-control, and finally felt ready to look for a healthy partner for life. Then Vanessa started to date Josh, whom she raved about. Although I hadn't met him, I knew that he was trouble simply by watching Vanessa's behavior. She was deteriorating; she was slowly reverting back to old addictive habits, and yet she was unaware of it. When I questioned her about who this young man really was, she reassured me that he was the most wonderful thing that had ever happened to her, and by far the most attractive man she had ever dated.

As Vanessa continued to deteriorate, I became increasingly

concerned. When I had an opportunity to speak with Josh on the telephone, my fears were confirmed. Even over the phone, I could tell that he was very unfocused, insecure, and ungrounded. After a long conversation with him, it became clear that he also had an addictive personality. But, unlike Vanessa, he had not begun to work on himself. Vanessa had overcome so much, yet when they met, he brought out her weaknesses. They connected at their lowest common denominator.

When I pointed all of this out to her rationally, Vanessa denied it. She simply didn't want to hear it. She didn't want to lose that blissful feeling she had – no matter how destructive it was. Then Josh started pushing her to get engaged. She wanted to, but a little voice inside told her to wait. She started to believe that there was a problem, but she decided that it was a very small one. Nonetheless, she agreed to meet with me, together with Josh. I spelled the issues out to both of them, hoping that he would agree to go for help, but instead, he fought with me and denied everything. Slowly, slowly, Vanessa opened her eyes and told him that he really did have an issue and that she would support him in working through it. He grudgingly agreed.

Off Josh went to the therapist. In the middle of the second session, he stormed out, saying, "I don't have any problems! You're all crazy!" Later that evening, he called Vanessa to meet up. He thought that she was going to break up with him because he refused to deal with his issues. So he broke up with her first. Afterwards, Josh called to tell me the news. He said, "I broke up with Vanessa because I thought that she would break up with me. But now I realize that she wouldn't have broken up with me. She's too weak to break up with me." He was really taking advantage of her weakness the whole time.

When Vanessa and Josh first met, they hit it off immediately.

However, the point of their connection was their weakness, not their strength. Vanessa had to shrink in order to be in a relationship with him. When she finally understood this, when she looked at herself and saw how much she had deteriorated, she gained the strength to walk away from him; only when she thwarted his many attempts to get back together with her did he finally get the message.

It makes sense that sometimes couples do connect at their lowest common denominator. Whether it happens consciously or subconsciously, you tend to connect to people who have experienced similar struggles and traumas. If you have both worked through these issues, it might make for a very profound relationship. But if the person you're dating has issues that are still haunting him or her, your connection can bring out the absolute worst in you.

We all have a part of ourselves that's more developed and mature. We also have our less developed, immature side which lags behind. I'm not referring to the silly, fun part of our personalities. The immature side is the part of you that is selfish, thwarts growth, and seeks instant gratification, even at other people's expense. The mature side of you, on the other hand, yearns to grow, to give, to reach your potential. If you were to think of the three most meaningful moments or experiences in your life, there is no doubt that your mature side would be at the forefront. It is the part of you that you respect, the part of you that is wise and yearns to learn from mistakes.

After the Josh episode, Vanessa strengthened her conviction to marry a man who brought out her strengths. Soon after, she met and married the most wonderful, warm, supportive man, who incidentally didn't have a struggle with addictions.

At one point early on in their marriage, Vanessa told me that she was struggling because she felt she couldn't really share all of her past issues with him. He had never gone through such things and couldn't fully relate. I explained to her that in order to be close to someone, you don't need to dig up your whole past *and* you don't have to share the same baggage. I suggested that she try to move forward and to focus on the greatness that he brought out and supported in her. She let the past go and moved boldly into the future. Today, she is a woman of tremendous strength and wisdom, helping many to overcome their own weaknesses. It is sobering to think about who she became and who she could have become had she not stepped up to the plate.

Another way to approach the same issue is to ask yourself, *"Do I like myself when I am with him or her?"*

Sometimes people say, "But I feel so good when I am with him/her." This doesn't prove anything. It could just be infatuation. The key question is do you feel good *about yourself* when you are together? When Joan Jett sings (in a popular song from the '80s), "I hate myself for loving you," she's expressing the type of pain that you want to avoid. You should love yourself for loving your mate. You should also love how you act when you're together.

If the relationship is a healthy, growing one, there will be times when you're challenged to change. For example, if you're habitually late and it gets on your spouse's nerves, you might be upset with yourself at those moments. But those are healthy moments of frustration that can propel you forward to make a real change. Those are what are aptly called growing pains. The type of pain you want to avoid is the pain of shrinking, the pain of losing your greatness. That's when you may not like yourself, when the other person brings out the "smallness" in you, your narrowness and immaturity. It could be your addicted side, selfish side, obnoxious side, needy side, or controlling side (you fill in the blank). When the relationship highlights a weakness, it's easy to stop liking yourself.

Another important question to ask is: *"Is the person you're dating throwing your life into chaos?"*

For example, are you suddenly failing your classes in school? Slacking off at work? Are all of your friendships starting to fall apart? A healthy relationship shouldn't throw off the balance in your life. A positive relationship should enhance your life. If you're excited about someone you recently met, you might have a harder time concentrating on your studies or perhaps be a bit less ambitious at work. But the change should not be a drastic one. And certainly not a negative or destructive one.

When I was in college, I had a classmate who was very bright and had fantastic leadership qualities. She was majoring in psychology and it was clear that she had a successful future ahead of her. Or so it seemed. She started dating a guy who really threw her life off course. Over the year, she started to slack off in her studies. The following year, she decided that she didn't want to be a social worker. But she couldn't figure out *what* she wanted to do. It was sad to see this ambitious, charismatic young woman lose her focus and direction in life. The strange thing is that the guy she was dating, who was also a psychology major, continued with his ambitions. By the end of her senior year, she graduated by the skin of her teeth, while her boyfriend got accepted into a top master's program. On top of everything, she also put on a lot of weight and stopped taking care of herself. I have no idea what transpired in their relationship that caused her to deteriorate to such an extent. The only thing I know for sure was that it wasn't a situation of abuse. It was much more subtle than that.

Unfortunately, this was not the last time I witnessed such a phenomenon. I have to admit that it is one of the most painful things to observe. The bottom line is that you have to genuinely ask yourself the following questions to make sure that you don't waste precious years and potential, swallowed up in the wrong relationship.

Three Essential Dating Questions

1. Does the person I am dating bring out the best in me? Does he or she bring out my more mature side?

2. Do I like myself when I am with him/her? Do I feel good about myself when we are together?

3. Is the person I am dating or the fact that we are dating throwing my life into chaos? Am I able to maintain the balance between the different interests and people in my life?

CHAPTER TEN

QUESTION #10:

If the person you are dating never changes,
would you still want to get married?

*C*ontrary to common belief, women do not have a monopoly on trying to change their spouses or potential mates. Men often fall into the trap of trying to change the women in their lives as well. Many people make the mistake of marrying with the hope that "the man I'm dating will change after the wedding" or "she'll change because she loves me." But the best way to ensure that someone won't change is to expect them to change. No one blossoms under such pressure and expectations.

We all have a tendency to rebel when someone tries to change us. The funny thing is that although we might be open to the natural process of change, once someone is breathing down our necks, we tend to shut down. Therefore, one of the most important questions to ask yourself before you make a commitment is, "If this person never changes, will I be able to love him/her as he/she is?"

One of my friends told me a hair-raising story about her cousin's marriage. She told me that her cousin, Samantha, was a very scholarly woman. She was bright, ambitious, and well read. Samantha was introduced to a man who was the sweetest guy she had ever met. He was one of those individuals whom everyone sincerely loved. They dated for a while and were crazy about each other. Although he was not an intellectual, she decided that his character was so outstanding that she would marry him anyway. But, after the wedding, his lack of intellect started to eat away at her. (For more on this kind of imbalance, see "Welcome to the 'Gap'" in chapter 6.) She tried to get him to read more, she made fun of his vocabulary, and put him down right and left. She was obviously hoping to push him into developing his more intellectual side. With each passing year of marriage, he became increasingly angry and resentful.

My friend and her cousin lived in different countries. So when they finally met again, ten years had passed. And that's when my friend got the shock of her life: Samantha's husband, who had been the epitome of sweetness, who used to look adoringly at his wife and dote on her, had become an angry, bitter, uptight man. She almost didn't recognize him! She was shocked to see what her cousin had done to this man, as a result of all of her negativity, constant insults, and badgering. I'll never forget the shock on my friend's face when she told me this story. It obviously made a tremendous impression on her and therefore on me as well. *When we try to change another person, we destroy the person we once loved and we destroy our relationship.*

When I tell this story during lectures, people always ask about habits that really do need fixing: for example, heavy smoking or eating junk food all day, etc. Is it okay to try to change one of these negative habits? Even in a situation where the person you are dating admits that this is a vice, he/she still has to want to change it for him/herself, not for you. If the person does want to change it, your encouragement could go a long way. It might even be what gets the person off the ground. But once your dating partner "takes off," he/she needs to run on his/her own engine, not yours.

A young man named Shawn once consulted me regarding his girlfriend, Cindy, whom he was planning on marrying after college. He had become more interested in religion, but was afraid to share his excitement about it because he didn't want to scare Cindy away. Even though they both shared the same religion, neither had been actively religious until now. Shawn really felt stuck because he didn't want to give up this great woman, nor did he want to squelch his spiritual needs. I explained to him that it wasn't fair to Cindy to hide his new interest. It also wouldn't be fair to expect her to jump on board. The healthy option would be to share the truth about his changes as well as his fears of losing her. He would then need to give her time and space to decide whether she would or could share his interests.

Shawn did just that. He gave Cindy time and space to search out her own religious convictions. Throughout that year, his girlfriend spent quality time learning and questioning her religious beliefs. By the end of the year, she told him that she too was inspired to grow religiously. Cindy explained that she needed that full year to discover this because she didn't want to change for him. She was trying to avoid the backlash that couples experience when they change "for the other."

This backlash is a serious thing. Take, for example, Cheryl, who once came to speak with me regarding her new marriage. She married Max, a man who loved the outdoors, hiking, agriculture, and farming. She was a city girl from a wealthy family. Although she enjoyed spending a week or so in the country, it wasn't where she felt at home. When she met Max, she was taken by how comfortable he was with himself. The other men she had dated seemed so bottled up and mechanical. Max had a natural flow and wasn't constantly trying to prove himself. Max also turned out to be a terrific salesman. He showed Cheryl the wonders of the country, and she was fascinated by what she learned about farming. Eventually, he succeeded in convincing her that she really was a country girl after all.

They got married and she was fine for about a year. After a year, she started missing her nice car and her comfortable, big house. Sometimes, all Cheryl wanted was to go out to a fancy restaurant or to order in some pizza. Even these comforts were missing in her new life. She started resenting Max, and their wonderful marriage turned sour. Cheryl felt that he had only showed her the pretty side of the country and had "conveniently" left out all of the dirt and the drab. In truth, he did leave out the negative side of the picture because he so wanted to marry her. She was also angry with herself for buying into Max's hard sell.

For a few months, they played a game of tug-of-war. Cheryl tried to pull him to the city. Max tried to pull her back out to the country. Before they knew it, they were in marriage counseling, trying to salvage their relationship. This is the type of backlash I was referring to earlier. In the end, they worked it out by moving to a beautiful suburban neighborhood, where they had a big backyard plus easy access to the nearby city. Max and Cheryl are fortunate to have worked it out. Many couples don't fare as well.

Although men have a tendency to try to change women, women are notorious for trying to change men. Often, a woman's desire to change a man comes from a good place: she wants to look up to him and therefore tries to turn him into the type of man she can look up to. But at the end of the day, it doesn't matter why she tries to change him. Her efforts will only create resentment and stress. If she continues to push the man she is dating to change, in the end, he probably will change, just not in the direction she had hoped for.

The irony is that only when people are accepted and loved for who they are will they be open to change. But the change has to come from within. People only change when they themselves realize the futility or destructiveness of their own behavior. I think that's true for all of us.

Our love and support can create a positive environment in which a person feels safe to change. The love and support must be unconditional in order to create this type of environment. You have to be ready to support and accept, and put your "change tools" back in the box where they belong. That is why it is so important to ask yourself the question, "If the person I'm dating never changes, would I marry him/her as he/she is today?" If you cannot accept the person unconditionally, without him/her needing to change something, start looking elsewhere for a spouse.

The joy of marriage can only be experienced when the couple are not trying to change or fix each other. The joy is experienced when you can love your spouse as is.

The Ten-Question Checklist

1. Do you share the same basic goals and values?

2. Are you relating to the person you are dating, or to an image?

3. Can you admit that the person you are dating has faults? Are you realistic about your own faults?

4. Does your relationship have healthy boundaries?

5. What do people you are close to have to say about the person you are dating?

6. Do you respect the person you are dating? Is there mutual respect?

7. Can you be open and honest with the person you are dating? Do you trust him or her?

8. How well do you get along with the person you are dating? How is your communication?

9. Does the person you are dating bring out the best in you?

10. If the person you are dating never changes, would you still want to get married?

CHAPTER ELEVEN

THE CASE FOR MARRIAGE

*W*ith the divorce rate soaring higher and higher, a common question asked by young women today is "Why bother getting married? It's probably not going to last anyway." A college student, Janet, once told me that her father (who was on his third marriage) had just given her a "pep" talk. He said, "I just don't want you to be naive. Marriage is not all that it's cracked up to be. It's great in the beginning but then it always turns out to be the same thing: You have your chores, he has his. You have your life, he has his. Marriage is just a convenience." With messages such as these floating around, it's not surprising that the institution of marriage is falling apart in today's society.

The saddest thing is that many people give up before they've even started. Others do want to marry, but feel ill-equipped and confused as to how to make it work. The previous ten chapters were focused on how to choose a marriage partner wisely. But in order to make your marriage work, you need more than just the right partner. You also need to know the elements necessary for a happy, healthy marriage.

Janet's father said, "Marriage is great in the beginning." After reading this book, you know exactly why. He's referring to infatuation, that temporary feeling that usually lasts less than three years. Infatuation can blind you and cause you to end up with someone who is not right for you. As a result, couples can end up feeling deceived and resentful, wondering, "Why and when did it get so hard?" Infatuation's effortless nature is what makes it so dangerous down the line. Because if you've never had to invest real effort or give of yourself, you won't have built any of the emotional muscles you need when infatuation wears off.

If you don't want to be another divorce statistic, if you do want to be a marriage success story, the first thing you need to internalize is that love is an activity: *it's a verb.* Although it is also a feeling, it is ultimately a verb. As Erich Fromm writes, "Because one does not see that love is an activity, a power of the soul, one believes that all that is necessary is to find the right object – and that everything goes by itself afterward. This attitude can be compared to that of a man who wants to paint but who, instead of learning the art, claims that he has just to wait for the right object, and that he will paint beautifully when he finds it."[17] If you're waiting for the "feeling" of love to hit you and then miraculously stick around forever, you're setting yourself up for pain and disappointment. *When those initial feelings of love start to fade, the only way to regenerate them is through loving actions.*

Infatuation is effortless; love takes work.

The "work" of love, if approached correctly, is beautiful and profound. It's work that will bring out your greatest human potential. People like Janet's father who mistake infatuation for love miss the point. Upon finding a hidden treasure chest, they revel in the treasure chest itself. They miss the point that the value of the treasure chest is *the treasure inside.* What is this treasure? Love. Why do so many people get stuck on the treasure chest (infatuation) and forget about the treasure? Let's see why.

---

17. *The Art of Loving* (New York: Harper and Row, 1956; repr. London: HarperCollins, 1995), p. 36.

Love Is a Choice

The human being is made of much deeper stuff than the base desires we all share. Infatuation is rooted in our lower self. Love, on the other hand, stems from our higher self, which is also where our ability to choose is rooted (I'm not referring to the choice of what we should have for breakfast; I'm referring to moral choices). Love is a choice. *When I say that love is a choice, I am not suggesting that you should pick out some random person, and choose to love and marry him or her. Obviously there has to be an emotional connection, attraction, shared values, respect, and all of the other things I've mentioned earlier in this book.* What I am saying, though, is that no matter how great your initial connection is with someone, those feelings will never just continue if you don't eventually choose loving actions. The potential and power of our ability to choose is immeasurable.

Attitude Is Everything

Even though we can't always control what happens to us, we can always choose how we will respond, as Francie Baltazar-Schwartz shows in this story:

Jerry was always in a good mood and always had something positive to say. When someone would ask him how he was doing, he would reply, "If I were any better, I would be twins!" Jerry was a restaurant manager, unique in his field, and even had several waiters who followed him around from restaurant to restaurant. The reason the waiters followed Jerry was because of his attitude. He was a natural motivator. If an employee was having a bad day, Jerry was there telling the employee how to look on the positive side of the situation.

Seeing this style really made me curious, so one day I went up to Jerry and asked him, "I don't get it! You can't be a positive person all of the time. How do you do it?"

Jerry replied, "Each morning I wake up and say to myself, 'Jerry, you have two choices today. You can choose to be in a good mood or you can choose to be in a bad mood.' I choose to be in a good mood. Each time something bad happens, I can choose to be a victim or I can choose to learn from it. I choose to learn from it. Every time someone comes to me complaining, I can choose to accept the complaints or I can point out the positive side of life. I choose the positive side of life."

"Yeah, right, it's not that easy," I protested.

"Yes, it is," Jerry said. "Life is all about choices. When you cut away all the junk, every situation is a choice. You choose how you react to situations. You choose how people will affect your mood. You choose to be in a good mood or bad mood. The bottom line: it's your choice how you live life."

I reflected on what Jerry had said. Soon thereafter, I left the restaurant industry to start my own business. We lost touch, but I often thought about him when I made a choice about life instead of reacting to it.

Several years later, I heard that Jerry had done something you are never supposed to do in a restaurant business: he left the back door open one morning and was held up at gunpoint by three armed robbers. While he was trying to open the safe, his hand, shaking from nervousness, slipped off the combination. The robbers panicked and shot him. Luckily, Jerry was found relatively quickly and rushed to the local trauma center.

After eighteen hours of surgery and weeks of intensive care, Jerry was released from the hospital with fragments of the bullets still in his body. I saw Jerry about six months after the accident. When I asked him how he was, he replied, "If I were any better, I'd be twins. Wanna see my scars?"

I declined to see his wounds, but did ask him what had gone through his mind as the robbery took place. "The first thing that went through my mind was that I should have locked the back door," Jerry replied. "Then, as I lay on the floor, I remembered that I had two choices: I could choose to live, or I could choose to die. I chose to live."

"Weren't you scared? Did you lose consciousness?" I asked.

Jerry continued, "The paramedics were great. They kept telling me I was going to be fine. But when they wheeled me into the emergency room and I saw the expressions on the faces of the doctors and nurses, I got really scared. In their eyes, I read, 'He's a dead man.' I knew I needed to take action."

"What did you do?" I asked.

"Well, there was a big, burly nurse shouting questions at me," said Jerry. "She asked if I was allergic to anything. 'Yes,' I replied. The doctors and nurses stopped working as they waited for my reply. I took a deep breath and yelled, 'Bullets!' Over their laughter, I told them, 'I am choosing to live. Operate on me as if I am alive, not dead.'"

Jerry lived, thanks to the skill of his doctors, but also because of his amazing attitude. I learned from him that every day we have the choice to live fully.[18]

Jerry shows us just how far-reaching our choices are. Here is someone who really understands the inner power of choice, of rising above our initial reactions. This attitude is directly linked to success in marriage. If you want to have a phenomenal marriage, the first thing that you need to internalize is that you have the ability to create that marriage, to choose to love. *The choice of love is to act lovingly: to give, to nurture, to support. To realize that when you give love, you feel love.* The treasure chest can only be opened when you realize that you have the power to choose love.

Bob was a man in a mediocre marriage. One day, he went to a lecture on marriage and found himself getting upset. He thought, "It's so sad that I'll never experience such a nice

---

18. In Jack Canfield et al., *Chicken Soup for the Soul at Work: 101 Stories of Courage, Compassion and Creativity in the Workplace* (Deerfield Beach, FL: Health Communications, Inc., 1996). Reprinted by permission of the publisher.

marriage. My wife just doesn't get it. I had so many visions for my marriage but we're so far from these hopes. I can't believe that I'm in this situation." Suddenly Bob caught himself! He thought, "Wait a minute, am I being the best husband that I can be? Am I the type of husband I had imagined myself being before I got married? No! Instead of blaming my wife and expecting her to turn around, I am going to turn around!" He went home with conviction: conviction that he was going to make his wife the number-one priority in his life. Conviction that he was going to be the husband that he had hoped to be, once upon a time.

He did just that. At first, his wife was suspicious. She didn't know what he wanted from her. But as he showered her with kindness and love, she in turn did the same. Within a year, he had created the marriage of his dreams. Until then, he hadn't realized the extent of the power of his choices.

Lauren, a student of mine, had grown up in a broken home. Her parents divorced when she and her siblings were young, and she barely had a relationship with her father. Her mother hated him very much and made sure that this hatred was inherited by all of her children. Lauren's mother had issues with men in general and this was the environment in which she grew up. When I met Lauren, she was very skeptical about marriage, and I understood why. She attended my classes on relationships throughout the year, and tried to reframe her vision of marriage. It wasn't easy, but she was persistent. About a year later, Lauren met a special young man. She immediately felt that she could trust him, but was still anxious about marriage. Nonetheless, as she got to know him, she realized that he was a man she could really build a future with. They continued dating and got engaged.

When I heard about the engagement, I was thrilled, but I have to admit I was also a bit worried. I hadn't seen her for a while and I hoped that she still maintained her healthy outlook. A few months later when she came to visit me with her husband, I was astounded. Not only did she marry an amazing young man, she was also building a model marriage. A few days later, I asked her how she did it. She answered, "I have conviction to be happily married. I therefore decided to do the exact opposite of what my mother did. That is my secret." There's the magic word again: *conviction*. Conviction means that you have the ability to choose your reality, and you are going to do just that.

My husband Aryeh also lectures on the topic of love and marriage. After one of his lectures, he was approached by a successful businessman, who said to him, "I wish that I had learned about the choice of love before I got divorced. I still love my wife very much and I realize that I made a mistake in letting her go. I thought that marriage and love just happened to people. I didn't realize that you're supposed to work on your marriage. No one ever spoke about that when I was growing up. I was busy with my job and when I stopped feeling excited about my marriage, I thought this meant that it was time to get out. Now I realize why my wife wanted to go for counseling, but it's already too late. She doesn't want to see me again."

When people make mistakes such as these, the scars are painful to endure. Love is a verb, it is an activity, it is making a choice. When married couples start complaining that they just don't "feel" the love anymore, it's typically because they're not making the right choices. It is also because they are not doing the right actions. Since love is a verb, a person must act lovingly in order to experience love.

What Are the Actions of Love?

Giving

The first action of love is giving. What comes first, giving or loving? Rabbi Eliyahu Dessler, a famous mid-twentieth-century Judaic scholar, taught that "We are accustomed to thinking that giving stems from love, because when we love someone we naturally give to them. But there seems to be another side to this argument." Rabbi Dessler goes on to explain that when we invest ourselves in someone or something, we come to love the person or thing we pour our love and attention into. As it says in the Talmud, "If you want to love your friend, give to him and nurture him."[19]

Although it's true that we feel like giving to those we love, if we always wait for that loving feeling to inspire us to give, we'll miss the boat of true love. We have to train ourselves to look for opportunities to give, even when we're not "in the mood." This is hard because we're all somewhat selfish by nature; throughout the day, our thoughts are constantly occupied by our wants and needs. In order to counterbalance this tendency you might want to try the following exercise, which is tried and true.

19. Rabbi Eliyahu Eliezer Dessler, *Michtav M'Eliyahu* (Tel Aviv: Ofist Re'em, 1987), p. 36.

Exercise: Giving

Set aside three minutes a day to work on giving. During these three minutes (be sure to time it), think only about one particular person you know. It could be your spouse, best friend, parent, sibling, neighbor, coworker, classmate, you name it. The person could be someone who lives in your neighborhood or on the other side of the globe. For three full minutes, think about this person's needs, what would make him or her happy, and what he or she might be going through.

Stay focused; you'll notice that your mind will wander back to your own needs every now and then. (It's amazing how difficult it is for us to get out of our own needs for even three minutes!) When you lose focus, simply bring your mind back to this person.

OPTIONAL: At the end of the exercise, look for a way to do at least one nice thing for this person. It might be something as simple as writing a short, warm email.

Do this exercise for one month and you'll notice a major difference in your thinking process. If you're married, focus exclusively on your spouse for three consecutive minutes a day for the whole month. This is crucial because we often tend to take those closest to us for granted. (If you are not married, you can focus on the same person every day or choose someone new). The women I teach are always amazed at how effective this one exercise is in creating a happier marriage. As one of the women said, "My marriage is really good. I didn't feel a strong need for improvement but I tried the exercise anyway. I can't believe how powerful it is. My already good marriage became great."

Why is giving so powerful? When we give, we connect to the highest part of ourselves; we connect to our intrinsic goodness. It's then that we remember that that's who we really are. When we disconnect from this goodness, we feel an emptiness inside of ourselves. From a Judaic perspective, this intrinsic goodness is the divine spark within us, or our "Godliness." A conversation I had with a young woman, Stephanie, exemplifies this. She was an exceptionally intellectual woman who was having trouble building an emotional connection with the man she was dating. When I asked her if she was a giver in the relationship, she answered, "I know that it's a good thing to give – I know that intellectually – but in reality I'm a taker."

As we spoke further, Stephanie explained to me that her parents had adopted a couple of children who had become her younger siblings. She had been a very studious teenager who didn't appreciate having these young, needy children around. She grew increasingly annoyed by them with every passing day and resented her parents for adopting them. Although she was never a big giver, now she retreated into her "space." Her mother tried to show her the positive aspects of giving and caring for others, but she closed down. Now, years later, this reaction of hers was blocking her from serious dating. She was absolutely terrified of marriage. She knew that she needed to change, but she didn't know where to start.

Stephanie made another appointment with me to finish our conversation. When we met, I showed her a paragraph in Erich Fromm's *The Art of Loving* that changed her life.

> The person whose character has not developed beyond the stage of the receptive, exploitative, or hoarding orientation, experiences the act of giving this

way [i.e., giving up something, being deprived of something, sacrificing].... For the productive character, giving has an entirely different meaning. Giving is the highest expression of potency. In the very act of giving, I experience my strength, my wealth, my power. This experience of heightened vitality and potency fills me with joy. I experience myself as overflowing, spending, alive, hence as joyous. Giving is more joyous than receiving, not because it is a deprivation, but because in the act of giving lies the expression of my aliveness.[20]

Once Stephanie read the quote she realized that she had gotten it all backwards. She was eager to improve herself, so I gave her exercises and reading material, and she was on her way to reframing her feelings about giving and marriage.

The real joy of giving is experienced when you give with no strings attached. If you give while waiting for "what's in it for you," you'll never experience this joy. As you develop your giving muscle, you can become proficient in giving what your mate needs or likes, not what pleases you. And when you free yourself from the prison of selfishness, you'll realize that the more you give, the more you have.

Gratitude

Another action of love is gratitude. It is so essential to get in touch with and express your gratitude. Every human being knows how it feels to give, yet to be taken for granted. It zaps the life out of us. And, as mentioned earlier, the people we take

---

20. *The Art of Loving* (New York: Harper and Row, 1956; repr. London: HarperCollins, 1995), p. 18.

most for granted are those closest to us. One of the pitfalls of marriage is that each spouse waits for their needs to be met, for what's "coming to them." This ungrateful, selfish attitude is what can dry up a potentially wonderful marriage.

Gratitude is not only important for the spouse who receives the "thank you." Gratitude is equally important for the spouse who gives the "thank you." When you are appreciative of what your spouse is doing for you and your family, you are filled with positive feelings. And the more positively you feel towards your spouse, the more you'll be able to open your eyes to the other wonderful things that he or she does. As you feel more grateful and express this gratitude, your spouse feels appreciated and desires to give more. This positive cycle is another one of the secrets hidden in the treasure chest. Unfortunately so many people are stuck in "me, me, me" mode that they're unable to benefit from this cycle.

Openness and Willingness to Change

An additional action of the verb *love* is being open to change. Although it's futile to try to change others, you should always work on improving yourself. We all have areas in our personalities that could use some fixing, such as a tendency to be messy, late, controlling, insensitive, or needy. It could also be selfishness, lack of receptivity, being critical, rude, or unforgiving. Whatever it is, if you don't address these flaws, they can make a real mess of your relationship.

A woman I know named Karen is a perfect illustration of this. She was in a very difficult marriage, so she went to a marriage counselor to get some help. There she explained her situation: "My marriage is on the rocks. My husband is an incompetent marriage partner; he's selfish, sloppy, and inconsiderate." The marriage counselor stopped Karen and asked her about herself. Karen told her about herself, and the counselor said, "If you want your marriage to work out, you have to work on your tendency to be critical and negative." Karen finished her session and left.

Ten years later, Karen went back to the same marriage counselor. She told her, "My marriage is on the rocks; my husband is obnoxious, arrogant, and messy." The marriage counselor stopped her and said, "Tell me about yourself." After Karen did this, the counselor said, "If you want your marriage to work, you have to work on your tendency to be critical and negative." Karen was amazed. The marriage counselor had told her to work on the same exact trait in her session ten years earlier. She turned to the counselor and asked her if she remembered her. The counselor said no. Karen then said, "I was here ten years ago and you told me to work on the exact same character trait. But that was my first marriage; this is my third."

The message from Karen's marriage counselor was that even though your husband might have objective faults, you also have your own set of faults. And your faults will get in the way of any healthy relationship you have. You can't change your spouse; you can only change yourself.

People bury potentially wonderful marriages because they are fixated on their spouses' faults. Yes, it is very hard to put up with certain things in a marriage partner. But we have to remember that our spouses are also putting up with difficult things in us. They're not perfect, and we're not perfect either.

The good news is that once people focus on their own growth, they are less bothered by their spouses' imperfections. This "small" change can alter one's entire perspective. Why? Why would focusing on our own growth cause us to be less annoyed by our spouses' flaws? When we try to change our own flaws, we are humbled for two reasons: we realize how hard it is to change, and we realize what our spouses are putting up with, in us.

Benji, a friend of a colleague, spoke with me about an issue in his marriage. He said that his marriage was pretty good, except for the fact that his wife had one flaw that drove him crazy. He said, "If she would just change this one flaw, we'd have the best marriage." He ended up going to a marriage counselor about this issue. When Benji told him the story, the man said, "It's not fair to demand that only your wife change a flaw. If you want to be fair, tell her that it's very important to you that she change a flaw. It's so important that you're also prepared for her to choose a flaw that *she* wants *you* to change (while she changes hers)."

Benji liked this proposition and approached his wife with the deal. She immediately agreed and said, "Okay, I want you to be on time." (Benji is always notoriously late.) He said, "Okay, I'll do anything in order for you to change your flaw." Two weeks later, Benji said to me, "I can't be on time – it's physically painful for me to be on time!" After some more time passed, Benji decided that he really did want to work on his lateness problem. He started to realize just how many people were annoyed with him because of this bad habit. Benji took small, steady steps towards change, and although the "deal" was off, his wife was so astounded by his attempts to change that she finally took steps to change her flaw.

When you focus on your own changes, rather than trying to change your marriage partner, you also allow yourself to accept your spouse. As a result, you create a safe place for him or her to grow. In such an environment, your spouse might actually change the very areas where you wanted to see change. And when your spouse sees you changing, it usually inspires him or her to change as well. It's a win-win situation; as we grow into a new and improved version of ourselves, we give our spouses the impetus and freedom to do the same.

When you realize that marriage is an incredible vehicle of personal change, in addition to all of its other benefits, you're freed up to grow into your potential. Only then will you be able to see that your spouse has traits and abilities that you don't have, yet need. Only then will you see how symmetrically you can complement each other's strengths and weaknesses. If a couple understand this perspective, then the longer they're married, the more they'll be able to reveal this profound symmetry.

A marriage is meant to be a dynamic process. The reason that goals and values are emphasized in chapter 1 is because the foundation of a marriage is built on these common goals. These goals and values create a vision that propel the couple forward in attaining their dreams. As they pool their abilities together, they pave a path they could never have traveled alone. Rather than allowing their differences to polarize them, they celebrate these differences. Instead of complaining about these differences, they're able to say, "You have something that I don't have, and we need that to get where we're going." Whether these are gender differences, personality differences, or cultural differences, they are all tools necessary to travel their unique path. When a couple internalize this truth, as years pass, the wife can say to her husband, "I'm amazed at who I've become because of you," and he can say the same. Not only have they evolved as individuals, they've also created an "us," a fusion of both of their unique gifts. This experience is so powerful that the thrill of infatuation is absolutely silly in comparison.

Creating an "Us"

As we:

1. Embrace personal change
(instead of trying to change our spouses)

We then:

2. Escape the destructive tendency
to pick at our spouses

Which in turn:

3. Frees us up to see just how
complementary our differences are

This allows us to:

4. Pool our different abilities together

→ Which then:

5. Propels us forward to achieving
our common goals and visions

When a couple builds their marriage on a strong foundation of shared values, giving, and commitment to personal growth, their differences actually enhance their relationship. A student of mine beautifully described the pleasure she had growing up, watching her parents skillfully embrace each other's differences.

She portrayed her mother as the energetic, charismatic, "life of the party" type. Her father, on the other hand, is quiet, solid, and more internal. When her parents were in a public setting, she would observe her father admiring his wife as she gracefully "worked the crowd." Simultaneously, she observed her mother (who so appreciated her solid, loving husband; he was her rock) admiring her husband, who would sit on the side, completely comfortable with himself.

Every couple has their own unique legacy of how they can blend their differences. Over the years, I have had the joy of watching so many couples "blend," the joy of seeing two beings come together, creating a spectacular jigsaw puzzle – each puzzle a unique, evolving masterpiece.

Commitment and Devotion

The last action of the verb *love* that is vital to a happy marriage is commitment and devotion. It is commonly said that love can only flourish if there's commitment. *The ultimate commitment is marriage.* The security that marriage provides allows us to completely let our guard down and be ourselves. The safety of a committed marriage nurtures mutual trust and sharing.

Some of you might be thinking, "But I know many marriages that don't seem very secure and safe." Unfortunately, so do I. This is because commitment in marriage has two levels: a body and a soul. The body of marital commitment is the marriage covenant, the official agreement. This level of commitment is important, but it's dry and stoic, not vibrant. What is the soul of marital commitment? It's the daily choice to recommit to one's spouse and to the marriage. It's the daily commitment to make the marriage work, to work through difficulties, to be there for one's spouse no matter what. This constant commitment is what creates a safe and secure environment. It is in this environment of safety and trust that the word devotion takes on new meaning.

Every human being has the constant choice to choose love, to choose dedication, to choose loyalty. We are not a collection of instinctual impulses. We are remarkable beings, capable of incredible achievements. One of these achievements is the choice of loyalty. The treasure chest can only be opened with devotion and loyalty, for they are the very essence of love.

The path of love is not effortless. But what is effortless is short-lived; it disappears as quickly as it appears. Does it take courage to ask the ten questions in this book? Yes. Does it take even more courage to answer them? Absolutely. Does it take even more courage to open the treasure chest, to choose love, giving, gratitude, change, and devotion? No doubt.

But if you do embrace these treasures, you will be wealthy. It is my sincere hope that you'll go for it! It's worth every bit of effort. I'll be rooting for you.

If You've Already Been Married Once

The divorce rate being what it is, you're in good company. You are also in a position to know what worked and what didn't work. The most important thing to know is that we are all human and that we can grow from the mistakes we make. Once again, the key word is *conviction*. Conviction to get it right next time. Conviction to milk this experience for all of the wisdom it contains. Conviction to heal the wounds that exist. Conviction to not allow these wounds to turn into invasive scar tissue.

The 10 questions in this book are designed to help you clarify whether there is real, lasting potential with the person you are dating. They are also designed to reveal any unhealthiness in your relationship. A healthy marriage has good boundaries and mutual respect, and brings out the best in each partner. Additional signs of a healthy marriage are the ability to see one's spouse for who he or she is and to accept that person; shared values; and the ability to get along with, communicate and be open and honest with one's spouse. If the person you are dating passes the "10 question test," your marriage will have all of these healthy aspects.

When you look back at your failed marriage, you will notice that many of these questions were not considered before you made your marriage vows. As you apply these questions to your last marriage, they will reveal the faulty foundation of that relationship. The *Metzudas David*, an eighteenth-century Jewish text, teaches that "The ultimate happiness is the resolution of doubts."[21] This means that the more clarity, the more happiness.

---

21. Rabbi David Altschuler, in his commentary *Metzudas David* on Proverbs 15:30.

As you gain more clarity as to what went wrong and why, you will gain more happiness, for now you are equipped with insight. This insight will illuminate the road to your successful future marriage. You are now armed with the clarity from your past mistakes plus the clarity you'll gain from asking the 10 questions in this book, before entering your next marriage.

In addition to using the 10 questions, don't forget to apply chapter 11, for no matter how compatible two people are, if they don't work at the relationship – if they don't choose love over and over again – they will not taste the joy of a truly loving marriage. Take heed from a wise divorced man who, when I told him I was writing this book, said, "Tell everyone that the key is to work on the marriage when it's good. Because by the time the couple is in trouble, sometimes it's too late to do the work."

I encourage you to move forward, wisely and courageously, because a lasting and successful marriage is within reach. Don't let the pain of the past paralyze you and hold you back from building the relationship you truly deserve. If you apply the information shared in this book, the tears you shed in the past will now be transformed into tools to help you to reap joy.